The World's
Best Fish Stories

Previous books by the author:

Lost Treasures in Australia and New Zealand
Guilty Wretch That I Am
Treasure Ships and Tropic Isles

THE WORLD'S
BEST FISH STORIES

KEN BYRON

TYNRON PRESS

© Ken Byron, 1994

First published in Britain in 1994 by
Tynron Press Ltd
Unit 3
Turnpike Close
Lutterworth
Leicestershire LE17 4JA
England

ISBN 1 85646 102 5

Illustrations & cover design by Virus Art
Typeset in Malaysia by Syarikat Cultural Supplies Sdn Bhd
Printed in Singapore by Chong Moh Offset Printing Pte Ltd

Acknowledgements

The stories in this book were gathered mainly from the following newspapers:

The Times (London)
The New York Times
The Argus (Melbourne, Australia)
The Sydney Morning Herald (Sydney, Australia).

My thanks are due to these newspapers for permission to quote from their reports. I am also indebted to the staff of the National Library of Australia, Canberra, particularly the staff in the Newspaper Room, for their assistance to me during my research; and to my daughter, Julie Byron, for her proof reading.

Author's Note

All the stories in this book are true. Scout's honour! Or at least they were claimed to be true by the people who reported them.

When selecting the stories, I interpreted the term "fish" very loosely to cover all aquatic animals, including mammals such as whales and dolphins, and even a bird – the penguin.

Ken Byron

*With grateful thanks
to*

Mustad™

for their kind support.

Contents

1. My Favourite Fish Stories

November, 1839

Newspapers in Great Britain reported a fascinating story about a gentleman in Christchurch who had a very unusual pet – an oyster of the largest and finest breed whose name was Oscar. Each day Oscar was treated to a dip in sea water and fed with a ration of oatmeal, for which he happily opened his shell. According to his owner, Oscar was an admirable pet in every way. Not only was he good company but he was also very useful. He was a good mouser. Up to the time of the above-mentioned report, Oscar had killed five mice by crushing their heads in his shell. *(1)*

I realise that journalists, like fishermen, have rarely been known to lie; nevertheless I must admit that I had some doubt as to whether the story about Oscar was true. Then I came across the following report in *The Times* of 15 August, 1919:

> Mr John Symonds, a fish merchant of Great Yarmouth, found on opening his shop yesterday morning that an oyster had a mouse tightly caught by the head. Apparently the oyster opened to feed and the mouse tried to eat the oyster, which, being alive, closed its shell and killed the mouse. *(2)*

So, the story about Oscar was probably true after all.

December, 1892

An equally extraordinary story was reported in America about a man named Ernest Rounseville, of the East Freetown Fish Hatcheries (Ma.), who was said to be raising two-headed trout. This startling story naturally excited quite a lot of interest, so *The New York Times* sent a reporter down to check it out. He found that the story was quite true.

Mr Rounseville talked freely about the project, which had engaged a good deal of his attention for the previous few years, and said that the breeding procedure was quite simple.

He explained that twin eggs are found in every 50,000 to 100,000 trout eggs. There are two varieties of twin eggs, however. In one type the fish comprises two trout, united like Siamese twins. In the other type there is only one body with two heads joined to it in the form of the letter V. The breeder has to study the development of the fish very closely to determine which type it is. Initially, the fish's body, or bodies, are delineated only by black lines and the heads by black spots.

The rearing of the twin-body type is comparatively easy, said Mr Rounseville. However, in regard to the single-body type, he had been successful in one way but unsuccessful in another. He had managed to raise the fish during the early stages of their development but had not brought them to full maturity. The difficulty was that the two heads fought each other. In fact, they fought so fiercely for every scrap of food that more often than not both heads would miss out on the morsel and, over a period of time, the fish gradually starved to death.

Mr Rounseville had only managed to raise the single-body type trout to about 3 inches in length. But he was confident of success ultimately. He had been promised a bonus of $500 if he were able to bring a specimen to full maturity.

(3)

February, 1929

Do fish think? Yes, they do, according to a London man, Mr F.A. Williams, who told an interesting story about his goldfish in support of his view.

Said Mr Williams, "Some years ago we kept several large goldfish in a glass tank which became frozen over. One day the frost formed delicate fern-like leaves of ice which enclosed the fish in frozen cells. They became so still and lifeless that we were alarmed. My father broke the ice and, lifting the fish out, poured a few drops of brandy down their throats. Next morning, which was milder, we were astonished to find them all in a row, motionless, pretending to be frozen in." *(4)*

May, 1936

Mrs Wallace Powell, a housewife of Washington, U.S.A., saved the life of her injured goldfish by sewing it up with needle and thread. The fish had been swimming serenely around its bowl when someone accidentally knocked the bowl off its stand.

The bowl shattered and a sliver of glass cut the fish so badly that it was almost in two pieces. "He was hanging together only by his

spine," said Mrs Powell. Showing remarkable presence of mind, she raced across the room, grabbed her sewing basket, whipped out a needle and thread and then proceeded to sew up the dying fish. "I just took plain stitches," she explained, "as if I were mending a pair of pants."

The crude operation took about five minutes, after which she placed the fish in another bowl and settled down to see what transpired. In less than an hour the goldfish was moving rather unsteadily around the bowl, propelled by small wiggles from his fins. Then he gradually regained the use of his tail. Next day he was swimming normally and within a week he was back to his old self, with all of his manoeuvrability. (5)

December, 1938

Two small boys and a passer-by once solved a huge problem that faced another goldfish, this time in Victoria, Canada. The story was told by Herb Warren, the then City Park Superintendent. He said the boys were playing in Beacon Hill Park when they noticed the goldfish splashing near the surface. The fish's problem was that he had two tails which were working against each other. One tail was in the conventional position whilst the other was situated near the head. The tail at the rear end was trying to drive him forward, but the tail near his head drove him backward, with the result that he was getting nowhere.

Mr Warren said, "The fish's plight was not noticed during the summer and fall because visitors tossed plenty of crumbs and other food into the water and the two-tailed fellow was lost among the others. When winter came the other fish dropped to the bottom of the pond for warmth."

The boys called for assistance from a man who happened to walk by. The stranger produced a penknife, cut off the troublesome forward tail and dropped the goldfish back into the water. Immediately, the goldfish swam merrily to join his fellows. (6)

4

June, 1956

An Australian aboriginal known as Gulley was paddling his canoe when he found that he was being chased by a 12-foot crocodile.

Gulley came from a mission station near Cape York, at the top of Australia. He had been out hunting and had killed two wallabies which he was taking home in his frail ti-tree bark canoe. The wallabies bled profusely and left a trail of blood in the water behind the canoe. No doubt this was what attracted the crocodile.

When Gulley first noticed the crocodile he was more than a mile from the nearest land and he began pulling toward it. He threw out one of the wallabies, but the crocodile ignored it and kept coming. Gulley threw out the second wallaby and paddled even harder. The crocodile sniffed the wallaby, then stubbornly continued after the canoe.

Although still half a mile from the shore, and with the crocodile 30 feet behind him, Gulley dived into the water and began swimming for dear life. When he reached the shore he looked back and saw that the crocodile had bitten the canoe in half and was still attacking it.

Gulley injured his foot slightly whilst scrambling ashore and was treated by Dr Timothy O'Leary, of the Flying Doctor Service, who later related the story. Said Dr O'Leary, "An extraordinarily smart man; I'd have stayed in the canoe." *(7)*

5

2. Some Big Ones That Got Away

October, 1848

The Times reported an amazing battle between the crew of the American sailing ship *Daphne*, skippered by Captain Mark Trelawney, and an enormous monster.

On 20 September the ship was at lat. 4 deg. 11 S., long. 10 deg. 15 E. when the strange animal was sighted. It was described as a huge serpent or snake, with a dragon's head.

Immediately the monster was seen, the men loaded a deck gun with spike nails and any other pieces of iron at hand and brought the gun to bear on their target. When they fired, the monster was only about 40 yards away and they scored a direct hit. The animal reared high in the air, then plunged violently. As the skipper manoeuvred the *Daphne* closer towards it, the serpent was seen "foaming and lashing the water at a fearful rate". It disappeared for a time when the ship drew near, but then surfaced again some distance away.

Apparently now intent on making its escape, the creature began swimming away rapidly. It swam beneath the surface most of the time but appeared every now and again and this enabled the *Daphne* to continue its pursuit. The ship's mate estimated that the animal was travelling at a speed of 15 or 16 knots. The *Daphne* continued the chase for as long as possible, but eventually, as the light faded, Captain Trelawney was forced to break off and resume his voyage.

The mate estimated that the monster was about 100 feet long. His description of it agreed in every respect with that given to the British Admiralty some time previously by the crew of the *Daedalus*, who had also encountered an unknown animal on the high seas.   *(1)*

April, 1883

The existence of a sea monster of a completely different type was vouched for by Captain Augustus G. Hall and the crew of the American schooner *Annie L. Hall*. On 30 March, 1883, while on the Grand Bank in lat. 40 deg. 10, long. 33 deg., they saw an immense turtle. The animal was so big that, at first, they thought it was a vessel bottom up. The schooner passed within 25 feet of the monster so that they had ample opportunity to study it and estimate its size by comparing it with the length of the schooner.

All who saw it swore that the turtle was at least 40 feet long, 30 feet wide and 30 feet from the apex of the back to the bottom of the under-shell. The flippers were 20 feet long.

Turtles are not normally noted for their ferocity, but the report stated that because of the animal's enormous size, "it was not deemed advisable to attempt its capture".   *(2)*

March, 1921

Florenz Ziegfield, Jnr, of show business fame, with six fishermen, fought a tremendous battle with a devilfish off Florida. Ziegfield was in *Sea Robin*, a speed boat, and he was aided in the battle by Captain Bert Hiscock and other men in a fishing boat.

Ziegfield was towed 17 miles out to sea by the devilfish and when he returned at about midnight a search party had already begun to look for him. During the battle the devilfish was harpooned four times and shot with an army rifle eight times. But, in the end, it escaped.   *(3)*

June, 1935

Captain Manuel Chalor, skipper of the fishing trawler *Nautilus*, told an exciting story, on his return to port on 19 June, 1935, about the desperate fight that ensued when a 15-foot, man-eating shark jumped into a dory with him. It happened off the New Jersey coast when Captain Chalor was fishing for bluefish. Two members of his crew were on board the trawler whilst the third was fishing from another dory.

Captain Chalor surmised that the shark was pursuing a bluefish when his dory crossed its path, that the shark attempted to leap over the dory but miscalculated and landed in it instead. The captain had been just about to haul in a large bluefish when he noticed a turmoil in the water a few feet away. Next minute, something very large, and grey in colour, flashed past him and crashed into the bottom of the boat.

"I didn't know what to do, for a moment," he said. "There was a 15-foot man-eater right in the boat with me, thrashing around like a trawler wheel and threatening to stave in the ribs. I tried to keep out of his way, but the fish was too big and the boat was too small. His jaws were snapping and I tried to keep clear, but in doing so I slipped. He got one of my arms in his mouth and I felt my skin rip.

"I had been yelling for help since he landed in the boat, but when he grabbed my arm I yelled louder. My dory was only about 15 or 20 feet from the trawler, so two members of the crew saw the shark and began to throw big pieces of timber and old iron at it. He finally slackened up on his grip and I ripped my arm clear.

"I was about to jump in the water to get away from him, but I finally decided I'd rather be in the same boat with a shark than in the water with him. I'm not such a bad swimmer, but I'm not that good."

For ten minutes the two crew members who were aboard the trawler kept yelling and throwing everything they could find at the shark. Captain Chalor said he was kept just as busy in endeavouring to dodge their missiles as he was in trying to keep out of the way of the shark.

He continued, "One of the men finally threw an old harpoon, which struck the shark on the head. He gave a big twist and suddenly went back in the water, almost capsizing the boat as he went. I don't remember ever being more pleased at anything in

8

my life. That was one fish I was glad to lose.

"I'd lost a lot of blood, and my arm was throbbing from the shoulder to the ends of my fingers, so I ordered the other boat in and we headed for shore."

Captain Chalor lost consciousness from shock and loss of blood before the trawler arrived back at its home port of Otten's Harbour. His right arm was ripped from the shoulder to the fingers. (4)

August, 1937

Charles Risley, of Indiana, was happy to let a big one get away on one particular occasion. He was hauling in a 12-inch bass from a drainage ditch when it flipped against a hornets' nest on a tree. Risley and his dog fled, leaving the bass to the hornets. (5)

May, 1938

A fisherman lost his life when a huge tuna pulled him overboard. Laureano Villareal, a Costa Rican, was a member of the crew of the tuna fishing vessel, *Bijo*, which was fishing off the Peninsula of Nicoya, when he hooked the giant fish and was pulled into the sea.

Senor Villareal was a strong swimmer and was able to stay afloat without any trouble while the boat was swung around to pick him up. However, just as the boat neared him, he screamed and sank. His companions searched fruitlessly for him for several hours. Schools of tuna are frequently followed by sharks and it is presumed that it was a shark that killed him. (6)

January, 1940

A really big one got away from a Swedish fishing cutter off Skaw during World War II. The skipper reported that while hauling in the catch, one of the wire ropes holding the trawl snagged a U-boat. The cutter had full steam up but, despite this, the vessel was pulled along helplessly for about five minutes, until the wire broke. The periscope of the submarine could be seen clearly. *(7)*

April, 1941

Marcell Wackenie, of Nashville, Tennessee, announced that apologies were in order to 14 unknown fishermen, the reason being that, while fishing in Indian Lake, he had hauled in a large spoonbill catfish which had 14 hooks in its mouth. *(8)*

October, 1950

Another "big one that got away" story was told by an angler at Svinge, Denmark. Not only did the fish get away but the fisherman lost his favourite rod as well. He had hooked a low-flying Danish Air Force training plane. *(9)*

April, 1955

A turtle saved its bacon, so to speak, by crying. It weighed 540 pounds and was on its way to Kuala Lumpur's fish market and, no doubt ultimately, to a large soup pot.

While being loaded onto a lorry at Teluk Anson, a riverside town in central Malaysia, tears began to stream from the turtle's eyes. Fortunately for it, many Chinese believe that being kind to a turtle brings good luck and there happened to be a crowd of Chinese near the truck. A collection was quickly taken up, which raised the sum of 17 Straits dollars, sufficient to buy the turtle. Then, a woman paid an additional 17 dollars to have it taken out to sea and set free.

A witness reported that the turtle turned its head around several times and nodded, as if in gratitude, as it swam out to sea. *(10)*

April, 1959

Gaima, a New Guinea native, fought hard for the big fish he hooked, but in the end it got away. The fish was a big devil ray and it towed him around Bubuleta Bay for four hours.

The battle was watched by Lance Wilkinson, of the nearby

Bubuleta Plantation, and about 200 villagers. Gaima hooked the devil ray at about 4.30 p.m. while fishing from his canoe, near the village wharf. The fish immediately took off, with Gaima hanging grimly onto the line, and soon the canoe was travelling at a fast rate of knots.

After a while the canoe disappeared behind an island. Then, 15 minutes later, it reappeared on the other side of the island. Round and round the bay went the canoe, with Gaima receiving a cheer every time the craft passed the crowd which had assembled on the beach.

Mr Wilkinson said, "At nightfall, a hurricane lamp was passed to him from another canoe so he could comply with the harbour master's laws for navigation lights. All that could be seen was the glow of the lamp disappearing and returning ... The watchers gradually drifted off home.

"Two natives rowed a dinghy out to help Gaima. The line was hauled in. When the fish surfaced a few yards from the canoe, its size awed Gaima and in his hurry to board the dinghy, he capsized the canoe. Scared of being in the water alone with the fish, he let the line go, but it was still tied to the canoe. When the fish swept off again the line came taut with a jerk and snapped." *(11)*

January, 1968

Don Heatley, a big game fisherman, had the fight of his life with a mighty fish that towed him and his launch 20 miles across the sea for 32 hours. It happened near Mayor Island, New Zealand, and the strangest thing about the encounter was that the fisherman never saw his opponent.

Mr Heatley said that the fish was like the one in Ernest Hemingway's *The Old Man and the Sea*. He would fight for a while, then sink deep down and rest for half an hour – then burst into life again. Heatley wore through three pairs of gloves while hanging onto the line.

It was 3.20 p.m. when he hooked the fish and the fight went on throughout the night and all the following day. Twice, Heatley brought it within 20 yards of the launch, but it did not surface on either occasion. Then, finally, at about 11.30 that night, the line broke.

(12)

August, 1968

A voracious fish, which lived in a lake in a zoo park near Northampton (U.K.) in the 1960's, proved too cunning for the scores of fishermen who hunted it. It was believed to be a pike, about 5 feet long, with an estimated weight of about 40 pounds, and had become a problem when it started leaping out of the water, savaging and eating geese and other waterfowl, including fully grown birds.

The manager of the zoo called on a Coventry skin diving club for assistance. They used nets to drag the lake but failed to catch the culprit. Their only catches during this operation were two small pike, each weighing about 2 pounds, and a 4-pound tench. *(13)*

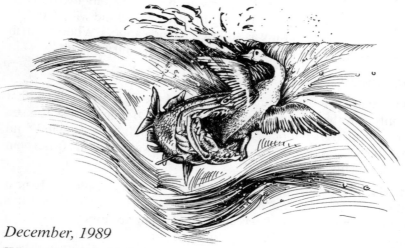

December, 1989

When 63-year old Bob Ploeger talks about his big fish that got away, one thing that he doesn't have to worry about is whether people believe him. His battle with the 100-pound-plus salmon that finally slipped off the hook was witnessed, not only by crowds of spectators, but by radio reporters, newspaper reporters and a television camera crew.

The battle began on 12 July, 1989 when Bob, accompanied by his wife Darlean and Dan Bishop, a guide, hooked a king salmon in the Kenai River in Alaska.

"It was a real hard bite," said Bob. "I let him take it, then I jerked the line to set the hook. I knew it was a big fish and it would take time."

The battle lasted for 37 hours. Sometimes the fish would lie motionless on the bottom; at other times it would race off at top speed, trying to escape.

The first time it leapt out of the water was one of the highlights of the contest. Onlookers were amazed at its size.

"I'd never seen one that big," said Bishop. He estimated that it was over 5 feet long and weighed more than 100 pounds – more than the existing 97-pound world record.

Ploeger and his two companions had to switch boats twice, the first time so that they could be in a boat with a motor, the second, so they could be in a bigger boat. But, throughout it all, Bob Ploeger retained the rod and reel. "I never slept – and I really didn't feel sleepy," he said. "This was the fish of a lifetime."

Finally, at 1.30 a.m. on 14 July, they tried to net the giant salmon. But he still had some fight left in him. With a quick jerk of his head, he broke free from the hook and was gone.

Bob was disappointed – naturally. But, judging by his comments, his disappointment at not catching the fish was overshadowed by his admiration for his victorious opponent.

"As that fish chugged slowly away into the river, I swore – then I silently saluted him. He'd fought hard and was still king of the river. That was one heck of a fish that got away." *(14)*

3. And Some That Didn't Get Away

August, 1860

The New York Times reported the following interesting account of the catching of a large muskellunge (muskie) near Clayton, on the St. Lawrence River:

> It is not uncommon to see little boys and girls on skiffs, rowing about the river, trolling. One day last week a small boy was thus engaged in the bay when he "fastened" to a mascalonge (*sic*). Being alone in the boat, with no implements to secure him or kill him, and the fish being as heavy as the boy, it was a fair and yet doubtful fight.
>
> The lad, however, had the advantage for a while; the fish grew weak from struggling, and the boy held his own. The boat swayed round and round as the fish struck out right and left, but at last the lad succeeded in getting Mr Mascalonge's head over the gunwale, and by some sudden convulsion of the fish he fell into the boat.
>
> And now the reader may suppose the fight was ended. Not so, for the boat sat low upon the water, and the 5-foot fish tried to leap overboard again. The boy let go his line and seized the fish around the body, and a rough and tumble ensued upon the bottom of the boat, first the boy being uppermost and then the fish.

The wrestling match was finally won by the boy, with the assistance of another fisherman who rowed up to them and towed the rocking boat ashore. *(1)*

August, 1907

There was great excitement at Virginia Beach, Va., when a swimmer decided to take on a shark. Fletcher Davis, a well-built young man from Oklahoma City, was a visitor to the area and was enjoying a swim when he spotted a shark in the breakers beyond

14

the safety ropes. He swam out and pushed and pulled at the shark until he got it within the ropes. This caused a panic among other bathers, of course, and there was a wild scatter for the shore.

Davis then grabbed the shark by the tail and dragged it ashore, to the wonderment of the crowd who watched his exploit. The monster was photographed, then weighed, tipping the scales at over 100 pounds.   (2)

July, 1922

Captain Hilding Swanson, skipper of a fishing vessel which operated out of Manasquan, New Jersey, dislocated his finger and two of his crew were hauled overboard during a battle with a 500-pound tuna.

The big tuna was the only fish in the pocket that day and the captain and his crew had a hard struggle to put a rope around its tail. But the tuna was still not finished. It hauled two men overboard and only succumbed when Captain Swanson struck it with an axe. The tuna was the largest caught along the shore that season and was placed on exhibition.   (3)

June, 1925

Two fishermen, Lester Wolcott and W.H. Bennett, fought for half an hour before they managed to despatch a shark and a swordfish which had been caught in their sea net about 20 miles off the New Jersey coast.

Each of the monsters was over 12 feet in length and they had been fighting each other before the fishermen arrived. The shark had been getting the worst of it.

Armed with pikes and axes, the two men attacked the antagonists, but this almost led to disaster because during the ensuing melee their boat was rammed and almost overturned. The net was badly ripped during the struggle and the smaller fish that had been trapped in it were able to escape.   (4)

July, 1927

A professional diver named Hook fought an eerie, hour-long battle with a giant octopus for possession of a human body. The incident occurred during the "hard-hat" diving era. Hook was engaged in the repair of a fishing net and was on the sea-bed at Port Townsend, Washington, about 50 feet below the surface. He noticed the octopus making its way across the ocean floor and was horrified to see that it had a human body in its clutches.

Hook was armed with a pike-pole so he advanced on the creature and attacked. Again and again he thrust the sharp pike at the octopus but it fought back strongly and held grimly onto its prey. At times the long tentacles threatened to envelope him. Eventually, Hook managed to pierce the body of the octopus, causing it to shrink back, apparently mortally wounded, and he was able to prise the tentacles loose from the corpse.

The body was later identified as that of the cook of a tugboat which had sunk in the harbour. Five crew members had drowned in the sinking and none of the bodies had been recovered.   *(5)*

February, 1931

In Tin Can Bay, Queensland, Australia, three fishermen were preparing for a restful night when they were suddenly galvanised into action by a most unexpected occurrence. They were lowering

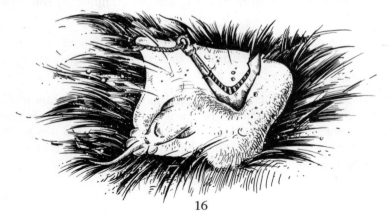

16

their anchor when a huge devilfish swallowed it and promptly headed for the open sea. Nothing they did seemed to have any effect in slowing down its headlong flight – even operating the motor in reverse. Eventually, however, the fish became exhausted and they were able to tow it back to shore. *(6)*

July, 1935

Turtles don't often come much bigger than the one captured by Captain Alfred Larson and his crew about a mile off the coast of New Jersey. It was a lagerhead turtle weighing 503 pounds and measuring 6 feet 4 inches across. The turtle was caught in the Bay Head Fishery's net and it fought for four hours before being subdued. It was claimed to be the largest of its kind ever taken in those waters and was shipped to a New York market. *(7)*

September, 1937

A party of shark hunters experienced 24 hours of non-stop excitement when they harpooned a giant basking shark off the west coast of Scotland. The shark was more than 30 feet long and was estimated to weigh 10 tons.

Three of the men were in a dinghy in Carradale Bay when they sighted the shark. They had been searching for a basking shark for nearly a fortnight because they were hoping to establish a plant in Scotland for the distillation of shark liver oil and they wished to ascertain whether this particular species would be suitable for the purpose.

When the harpoon struck, the shark took off at high speed, dragging the dinghy behind it. For several hours it followed a wildly zig-zagging course in the waters between Arran and the Mull of Kintyre. The rest of the party were in the *Myrtle*, a converted patrol boat, and in this vessel they were able to follow behind the dinghy. They even managed to change over the crew in the dinghy to enable the original occupants to have a rest.

It was hard work for the men in the dinghy – and dangerous.

They were constantly in danger of being overturned and they dragged on the rope continually, trying to control the shark's movements.

Night fell and the battle continued in brilliant moonlight. When dawn broke the shark was still fighting strongly for its life.

Then a fire broke out on the *Myrtle*. When the crew eventually managed to extinguish it they found that the dinghy was nowhere in sight. A call went out for help. Other ships were asked to keep a lookout and three planes began to search, also a lifeboat.

The dinghy was finally found by the lifeboat. The crew were exhausted, having been in the dinghy for 20 hours. The shark was also exhausted. It was lying still in the water. The harpoon line was attached to a buoy and the shark was later towed to shore.

It was estimated that during the 24 hours the dinghy had been dragged more than 100 miles.   *(8)*

December, 1949

Two men and a woman were in a 16-foot fishing dinghy off Seaholme, Victoria, Australia, when they were unceremoniously joined by a 9-foot grey nurse shark which leaped into the boat with them.

The unfortunate people concerned were Doug Miller, Fred Gay and Edna Martin. Even before their terrifying experience began, two members of the party – Miller and Martin – were unhappy. They were sea-sick and were not enjoying their day out on the ocean waves at all. Doug Miller was so sick that he was lying on the bottom of the dinghy. Then, a shark plunged over the bows of the craft and landed on top of him.

He suffered a badly-bruised arm and a few cuts during the ensuing affray. Said Miller later, "One minute I was lying there wishing I was dead. I felt terrible. Suddenly I heard a scream from Edna and a yell from Fred, and the shark landed on me. I didn't know what it was for a second. I nearly blacked out. I fought to get to my feet and as soon as I did, I was knocked down by its tail. Three times I stood up and each time I was knocked down. I felt like going overboard, but I knew I couldn't leave the other two. While I was fighting to get my balance, Fred was belting away at the shark with the smashed tiller. He was hanging on to Edna with one hand."

Fred Gay was an experienced fisherman and he said he had heard that the best way to stun a shark was to hit it on the nose. "Thank heavens it worked this time," he added.

Edna Martin said, "It was horrible seeing the shark threshing around on top of Doug, but it cured my sea-sickness. I'll never go fishing again."

The final killing blow was delivered by Fred Gay, with the remains of the tiller. A fishmonger bought the shark, which weighed 400 pounds. *(9)*

April, 1950

Ben Smith, of Gloucester, Massachusetts, had no need to talk about the big ones that got away. On just one day he caught four tuna weighing 290, 554, 580 and 588 pounds respectively. *(10)*

"Wish They'd Got Away!"

There have been occasions when fishermen would have wished that their big "catch" had got away. In November, 1952 the Brixham (U.K.) trawler, *David Allen*, towed for five miles a torpedo which had got caught up in its net. The crew managed to release the deadly missile into the water and, a few seconds later, it exploded, shaking the vessel badly. *(11)*

Another British fishing vessel, with the unusual name of *Why Worry?*, was ordered to stand offshore on 18 May, 1958 when the crew reported that they had a 1,000-pound magnetic mine caught in their net. Authorities decided to explode the mine at sea, but it turned out that the fishermen were mistaken. Investigations on the following day proved they really did not have any reason to worry – the object was a harmless compressed air cylinder from a torpedo. *(12-13)*

A Lossiemouth (U.K.) fishing boat, *Girl Freda*, netted a submerged submarine in the Moray Firth in September, 1959. *(14)*

Real danger threatened on 6 June, 1963 when the British fishing vessel, *Florence Harvey*, picked up in its net an unexploded 500-pound bomb which was later safely detonated by the authorities. *(15)*

April, 1954

An octopus picked the wrong man when it fastened its tentacles onto James Antone as he swam past some submerged rocks off Santa Rosa, California. Mr Antone was a big man of about 280 pounds and with arms more than two feet long. He used his weight and strength to pull the octopus free of the rocks, then simply walked ashore and beat it to death against a rock.

Mr Antone said, "I was in about 6 feet of water when I felt something like a muscled piece of wire wrap around my left arm. As I reared back another tentacle attached itself, and then another, another, and another. It was useless to try to tear the tentacles away, so I braced myself, heaved and ripped it away from the rocks. Its head was like a balloon and it kept spitting water all over me as I walked to shore with it."

It weighed 40 pounds and had tentacles 5 feet long. *(16)*

November, 1959

A 32-foot, 5-ton whale shark was caught by 16 fishermen from Mangalore, India, operating from two boats in the Arabian Sea. The men were working as one fishing party, but using two steel boats, one 32 feet long and the other 37 feet.

The story was told by Mr G.S. Illugason, who was training the fishermen for the United Nations Food and Agricultural Organisation. Mr Illugason said that the shark was sighted swimming on the surface and, after manoeuvring the boats alongside it, he jabbed a 30-inch unbarbed hook through its dorsal fin.

"Our two boats were roped together and both the engines stopped, yet the shark towed both boats at five knots," Mr Illugason said. "In a great fury the shark threshed and plunged and dragged the boats for 20 minutes. Then the two-inch manila rope parted and the shark swam off."

Later, the shark surfaced again and Mr Illugason managed to get a nylon line through the hook's eye. Then he and his men used a winch to secure the shark's tail to the bow of their craft and they towed it to Mangalore where thousands of people flocked to the wharf to see it. *(17)*

November, 1960

Two men at The Entrance (Australia) hooked a large eel which put up a tremendous battle during which it savagely attacked their 12-foot rowing boat.

They were using a flathead bait with a 12-pound breaking strain line. After taking the bait, the eel towed the boat more than half a mile. The fight lasted for 45 minutes. When brought alongside, the eel lunged at the boat and inflicted two 6-inch wide bites on the wooden hull with its razor-sharp teeth. Fearing serious damage to their boat, the men battered the eel with the long wooden handle of their landing net. In its death throes it bit five inches off its own tail.

Local fishermen identified their catch as a silver eel, a species that is usually found in tropical waters. It was 5 feet 6 inches long and weighed 33 pounds. *(18)*

May, 1967

Mr Bernard Venables, writer and keen fisherman, considers that his one lonely distinction is that he has had a tooth knocked out by a shark.

He was fishing off Gibraltar with two friends when he had a bite from a 143-pound shark. While Mr Venables continued to hold the rod, his friends rolled the shark into the boat.

"It is very unwise," said Mr Venables, "to bring a shark of that size into a small boat – ours was only a 24-footer. But they got it in. And then it suddenly became very active. The back end hit one of my friends on the leg, so that he had to go straight to hospital. The front end gave me a wallop on the head and knocked my pipe out of my mouth.

"At the time I was chiefly concerned that I was going to lose the pipe. (He recovered it.) It was only when I got back and looked in the mirror that I realised I'd lost a tooth. Right in the middle, I'm afraid." *(19)*

(One of Mr Venable's many books is entitled *The Gentle Art of Angling.*)

June, 1977

This is a story about a very hungry perch which lived in a pond owned by Mr Alf Leggatt, a former trawlerman, of Ickham, near Canterbury (U.K.). According to Mr Leggatt, the perch had become quite a problem. Over a period he practically emptied a pond of nearly 3,000 goldfish.

In June, 1977 his fantastic banquet was brought to an end by two men from the Southern Water Authority. Using electric shock equipment, they stunned and captured him.

Mr Leggatt said he would keep the perch but would house him in a separate pond. *(20)*

January, 1979

Ice-fishing is popular in some parts of the United States, also in Canada, of course, and a psychologist might find the sport an interesting field of study because of the insight it gives into the level of a person's optimism. You have to drill a hole in the ice before you can start fishing and the size of the hole shows just how much of an optimist you are.

Most fishermen drill a 6-inch hole. Dave Erlanson, who told his story to *The Washington Post*, was a born optimist. He customarily drilled an 8-inch hole. However, as we shall see, there was one occasion when even he was not sufficiently optimistic.

Erlanson explained that when a fish is initially hooked in winter, he doesn't fight much. It's just like hauling in a log when you first bring him to the hole. But, when he looks through the hole and sees your face in an eyeball-to-eyeball confrontation, he suddenly comes to life in no uncertain manner.

On the memorable day when Erlanson hooked his big one – New Year's Day of 1979 – in north-western Pennsylvania, he saw the red flag on his tip-up rig flip up and, racing to the hole, he grabbed hold of the line. He knew it was a big one immediately; he could feel its great weight. But he didn't realise what a monster it was until he saw the enormous head through the hole.

Then the fish took off. Erlanson played out 30 yards of 50-pound line through his gloved hands. The fish stopped and Erlanson brought it back to the hole again.

Three times Erlanson went through this procedure, but when he brought the fish back to the hole for the third time he knew it was played out. Then he found that he had a problem. He could not get the fish's head through the hole.

Two nearby ice-anglers helped him out. They drilled a second 8-inch hole and chipped out the bridge between the two holes. Then, after a lot of heaving and puffing, they managed to haul the fish out onto the ice.

It was a great northern pike measuring 46 inches and weighing a little over 29 pounds, a state record size.

One of the jokes ice-fishermen tell is about their fishing brethren further north who relieve the boredom between bites by catching polar bears. The procedure is quite simple. First you cut a hole in the ice. Then you put a ring of peas around the rim of the hole. You sit and wait. When a polar bear comes up for a pee, you hit him with a paddle. *(21)*

1982

Two solicitors from Darwin, Australia, sailed to Bathurst Island one day in a trimaran to try their luck. Initially, they were a little disappointed because their only catch in the first few hours was one small shark. They tethered it between the hulls of their yacht, then settled back to relax for a while and have a few beers. Their emergency craft, an inflatable rubber dinghy, was drifting at the end of a rope behind the yacht, a detail which happens to be important in this story.

Suddenly, they got the shock of their lives when the yacht was violently shaken and there was a series of splashes and loud noises. When they investigated they discovered that a huge shark had charged in, cut the small tethered shark in two, banged into the hull of the yacht and then leapt madly into the air.

By pure chance he came down right in the inflatable dinghy and, despite his enormous size and strength, he could not get out of it. He leapt and struggled but every time he fell back into the boat. He was still there, dead, when the fishermen sailed home. *(22)*

August, 1986

Donnie Braddick, a charter boat captain, caught his big one in the Atlantic Ocean about 25 miles south of Montauk, Long Island. It was a great white shark which weighed 3,450 pounds.

Thousands of people filed past to view the real-life "Jaws", which was caught on the bait of a whiting and fought for about two hours before being landed.

"The great white is the largest, meanest, nastiest, most unpredictable creature in the ocean," said another charter boat captain, as he gazed at the monster. *(23)*

4. Queer Fish

August, 1801

A very queer fish was reported to have been killed at the Madeira Islands near North Africa in May, 1801. Its length was measured as 56 feet 7 inches. Its girth could not be accurately measured because the body had sunk too far into the sand, but the diameter of the body was estimated to be about the same as, or more than, its length. The creature's tail was about 12 feet broad at its extremity and the jaw was about 8 or 9 feet long.

The report stated that "it had large teeth in the under jaw, with spaces between each tooth, but no teeth in the upper jaw, which was only full of sockets to receive the teeth of the under one".

The monster had been seen about the area for some time and when it came ashore, alive, the inhabitants set upon it and killed it.   *(1)*

November, 1850

A fish that makes a loud purring noise was caught off Brixham-roads (U.K.) and taken to Billingsgate market. Whilst not familiar to local fishermen, it was identified as a maigre (*scioenaquila*) and said to be common in the southern Mediterranean and off the shores of Spain and Italy, where it is considered to be a great delicacy. It grows to a large size, the one that was the subject of this report being between 5 and 6 feet long and weighing over 100 pounds.

The maigre swims in shoals and the purring noise is loud enough to be heard from a depth of 20 fathoms.   *(2)*

November, 1867

The oulachon, or candle fish, which is abundant in British Columbia waters, has always been extremely useful to Indians who lived in the area because it has served them, not only as food, but also as a source of light. These fish grow to about 10 to 12 inches in length and are remarkable for the high proportion of oil in their flesh. Despite this, however, the fish has a delicate flavour.

Piles of oulachon are dried in the sun, the oil that runs out being collected for cooking purposes.

To make candles, the Indians take a strip from the inner bark of the cyprus tree and, using a long needle made from hard wood, draw it through a dried fish. It is said that anyone could read comfortably by the light from such a "candle". *(3)*

July, 1877

William Todd went home after a day's fishing in the Tennessee River, leaving his line out. Next day it was gone.

A few days later a man named Elkins came across the line about a mile downstream. He and some friends followed the line and found on it a hideous monster which they pulled out of the water for close examination. It was dead, but it had not bitten at the bait; instead, the hook had caught in its body and in struggling to get free it had got the line wound around itself and drowned. In its struggles to get away, it had dragged a 40-pound sinker more than a mile.

The creature was 6 feet 7 inches long, weighed about 150 pounds and had a nose like a hog and a forked tongue. They supposed it to be some kind of sea shark, alligator, or alligator gar. *(4)*

April, 1883

In a letter to *The Cleveland Herald* (Ohio) Mr William C. Howells referred to a report on "singing fishes" in India which, he said, did not appear to have been taken seriously by anyone and he went on to say that the United States has its own singing fishes.

Said Mr Howells:

> Singing fishes was one of the first things I remember to have heard mentioned as belonging to the Ohio River. I heard it

said when I was a child and in the faith of childhood listened when I first came to that stream for the song of these fish, yet I seldom heard it, though old boatmen spoke of it in the quiet days of the flat-boats as quite common. One evening ... I heard the singing of the fish as distinctly as could be wished.

One afternoon, late in the summer of 1837, I stepped on to a flat-boat then used at Martin's Ferry, opposite Wheeling, West Va., when I was attracted by the sweet Aeolian harp-like sound arising from the water. I had forgotten the singing fish and asked the ferryman what it was. He replied as if speaking of a common matter, saying that it was the white perch, which followed under the boat back and forward across the river at that season when the water was warm and low. He was thoroughly posted in the habits of the fish, being bred to the work of fisherman and ferryman, and intelligently described the habits of the white perch of the Ohio, which, he said, had always been noted for this habit of singing.

I might mention, historically, that my informant was Ebenezer Clark, a son of Elizabeth Zane, famous as the heroine who, at the siege of the fort at Wheeling, carried the powder to the fort through a shower of Indian bullets. This does not materially affect the musical fish. I believe he gave me a correct account of the singing fish. I listened to their music while he told me about them. The sound was very much like that produced by a silk thread between the meeting rails of a window, sometimes called an Aeolian harp. If the perch can sing in Ohio, he may in India. (5)

August, 1906

Dr A.J. Butler, an experienced fisherman, saw such a strange sea creature off Berry Head (U.K.) that he wrote a letter to *The Times* in the hope that someone would be able to identify it. A lively controversy ensued during the next couple of weeks.

The fish was swimming on top of the water about ten yards away, so Dr Butler had a good view of it. He described it as being "about 6 feet long, 4 or 5 inches broad, tapering to about 2 inches at the tail, and quite flat – like a long, broad sword-blade. It was not more than an inch in thickness and of a buff colour. The edges were serrated and gave the impression of being set all along with tiny fins. As it plunged it reared two or three feet of its tail in the air and struck the water with resounding force". *(6)*

Mr Stuart Moore suggested that "it was an old basking skate. That is just what it would look like and just how he goes down with a flop of his tail. In hot weather these fish are frequently seen basking on the surface and I have had good sport hooking them with a long gaff. They are often 6 feet long and more". *(7)*

Another correspondent, Dr A. Gunther, suggested that what Dr Butler saw was a ribbon fish (*Regalecus*). "These fishes live at the bottom of the sea, generally at great depths, and very rarely come to the surface, except in consequence of some accident or after severe storms. Dr Butler's report renders it probable that the specimen seen by him was engaged in a struggle with some enemy." *(8)*

Dr Butler wrote to *The Times* again, obviously very irritated by the views of the first correspondent, but happy to accept the second suggestion:

> Mr Stuart Moore must not expect me to treat seriously his somewhat naive suggestion that the fish which I saw was a common skate basking. There is not the smallest resemblance between the two animals. I have little doubt that Dr Gunther's conjecture is correct and that what I saw was the rare *Regalecus Banksii*. The same conjecture was made to me by Mr Crawshay, of the Maritime Biological Laboratory, quite independently, and before Dr Gunther's letter appeared. Mr Crawshay adds that the *Regalecus* appears to be recorded only once on the south coast, and that in 1788. There is, therefore, sufficient warrant for regarding my record as of some scientific interest. *(9)*

May, 1913

A most intriguing report on a strange aquatic animal was published in an Australian newspaper, *The Argus*, on 26 May, 1913:

> Hobart, Sunday – The Secretary for Mines (Mr Wallace) received from Hartwell Conder, State mining engineer, a description of a remarkable animal reported to have been seen on the West Coast by some of the men engaged in State prospecting work that was being carried on in the little known country between Macquarie Harbour and Port Davey.

"I have to report," he says, "the discovery of an animal on the sea coast, about 12 miles north of Point Hibbs, of so strange a character that it is deserving of special mention. It is so strange that both the men who saw it and I myself anticipate quite cheerfully the smiles of incredulity of those who read this account. No one is asked to believe it.

"The animal was seen by Oscar Davies, foreman prospector, and his mate (W. Harris), who are working under myself, the State mining engineer for Tasmania. I have known both of them for a considerable number of years, and can guarantee absolutely their sobriety, intelligence and accuracy.

"They were walking along the coast on April 20 just before sundown on a calm day, with small waves rolling in and breaking on the shore, when at a distance of about half a mile they noticed a dark object under the dunes, which surprised them by showing movement. They advanced towards it and finally came within gunshot. When about 40 yards off it rose suddenly and rushed down into the sea. After getting out about 30 yards it stopped and turned round, showing only the head and a portion of its neck. It waited there for about five seconds, and then withdrew under the water and disappeared.

"The characteristics are summarised as follows: It was 15 feet

29

long. It had a small head, only about the size of the head of a kangaroo dog. It had a thick arched neck, passing gradually into the barrel of the body. It had no definite tail and no fins. It was furred, the coat in appearance resembling that of a horse of chestnut colour, well groomed and shining. It had four distinct legs. It travelled by bounding, i.e. by arching its back and gathering up its body, so that the footprints of the fore-feet were level, and also those of the hind-feet. It made definite footprints. These showed circular impressions, with a diameter (measured) of 9 inches and the marks of four claws about 7 inches long, extending outwards from the impressions and away from the body. There was no evidence for or against webbing. The footprints showed about 4 feet between the marks of fore and hind feet, and then a gap of about 10 feet, making a total of 15 feet. Laterally they were 2 feet 6 inches apart.

"The creature travelled very fast. A kangaroo dog followed it hard on its course to the water, a distance of about 70 yards, and in that distance gained about 30 feet. When first disturbed it reared up and turned on its hind legs. Its height, standing on the four legs would be from 3 feet 6 inches to 4 feet.

"Both men are quite familiar with seals and so-called sea leopards that occur on this coast. They had also seen before and subsequently pictures of sea lions and other marine animals, and can find no resemblance to the animal that they saw.

"Such are the details. When the humorists have enjoyed themselves at our expense the men of science may be able to connect this account with others which have come forward from time to time of strange beasts in our oceans.

"That no imprint was taken of the footprints and no marking out made of the form in the sand, no one regrets more than we do. The next tide swept over them, and they are gone." *(10)*

September, 1922

A very weird fish was scooped out of the water at Blue Point (U.S.A.) by Mr Clarence Seaman, of Patchogue. It was described as being about 4 inches long, with one eye, a head like an owl, three tails, which it wiggled all at once, and possessing horns all over its body.

Its reaction to being caught was no less strange than its appearance. It got so mad that it blew itself up, whistled three times, then expired.

Mr Seaman said that he would take the fish to the Aquarium in New York. No doubt its pickled body is still there today, residing in a jar somewhere in that institution. *(11)*

July, 1925

Dr William Beebe, a scientist, completed a marvellous scientific venture when he returned to New York after a 20,000-mile voyage in the *Arcturus*. Dr Beebe was accompanied by 13 other scientists, each of whom was a specialist in a particular field.

The expedition studied numerous marine mysteries and returned with thousands of specimens of aquatic life, some alive, some dead. These included about 50 new species and among them were some very queer fish indeed.

One fish had a transparent pane over its stomach, a kind of bay window which enabled an observer to see everything it had eaten and actually watch the digestive process in action. As well as its unusual stomach, this fish had an enormous mouth with distensible jaws and an expandable stomach, all of which gave it the ability to swallow and digest prey several times its own size.

The scientists reported that many deep-sea fish had their own built-in lighting system. In the darkness they appeared to be studded with glowing emeralds and sapphires. However, the lights always disappeared when the fish died.

There was great variety in the lighting systems of these fish. Some had only one or two lights; some had torches at the end of "fingers"; some had rows of lights. "One specimen emitted light through practically every pore," said Dr Beebe. "I'd say it carried 500 lights. You could not count them. It might have been 5,000. It was covered with tiny pin-points of light." Another species had headlights and tail lights, somewhat like an automobile.

One surprise was the discovery that the myctophids used lights to announce their sex. The males carried one light and the females two. In some species this was reversed.

Specimens taken from very deep water usually died immediately from the "bends", that painful affliction so feared by human divers. The change from extreme pressure at great depths to the weak pressure near the surface caused compressed or dissolved gases in their bodies to burst out as they expanded.

Among the curious marine insects that were studied were the halobates, insects with long legs which walk on the water and yet never get their feet wet. And, what is equally strange, although they spend their lives on that element, one drop of water on this insect's back causes it to immediately sicken and die.

The reason the halobates manage to keep their feet dry is that they are so light that they are supported by the surface tension of the water. Dr Beebe proved by experiment that a drop of water on the back of a halobate invariably proved fatal. So how do they survive when it rains? Are they able to dodge the rain-drops? No one was prepared to hazard a guess on that one.

As well as marine life, Dr Beebe's expedition also studied the ocean floor. They dredged up many specimens from a spot 100 miles from New York where the Hudson River once thundered over a giant waterfall. "The old river bed could plainly be seen," said Dr Beebe. That was two million years ago, since which time glaciers have changed the topography of the area completely. The waterfall was 930 feet, higher than any waterfall that exists on the earth today. *(12-13)*

October, 1927

Captain George Perry, of the *Marjorie Parker*, a keen fisherman, got quite a surprise when he pulled in his trawl line whilst the schooner was proceeding up the South Channel in Boston Harbour. On it, he had a haddock with three eyes. There were two normal eyes, with a third eye midway between them. Captain Perry said he would have the fish mounted and give it to a museum. *(14)*

October, 1927

A strange sea monster was washed up on the shore at Old Bar, a seaside resort town 10 miles from the New South Wales (Australia) town of Taree. It was found by Mr Thomson, a school teacher who was on holiday in the area, and was subsequently examined by dozens of people, none of whom had the faintest idea as to what species it might be.

It was estimated to weigh about 15 hundredweight and was described as follows:

The head resembles that of a bullfrog. It has large eyes, a very small mouth, and no teeth and no tail, but the hind extremity is rounded. Its hide is very thick and coarse; one fin protrudes from the back, while a corresponding one is on the belly.

These fins are each about 3 feet long. On the sides are two small flaps like elephant ears. *(15)*

May, 1929

A fish with a human face was reported to have been found by Julius Gabriel, a cobbler and spare-time fisherman, of Allentown, Pennsylvania. Mr Gabriel said the face was "slightly mongoloid and a bit weird, but none the less a face".

More than 2,000 people saw the fish, including academic staff from Muhlenburgh University, but there was no consensus as to what type of fish it was. Some thought it was a skate, while others believed it to be a ray.

Mr Gabriel was a bit upset about his find. "I think I had better stick to my last," he said. "On the next cast I might catch the devil himself instead of one of his assistants."

The New York Times gave the following description:

The creature has a large mouth, the interior of which is much like that of a human's. It has what appears to be eyes properly set with respect to the mouth, and a suggestion of a nose. The broad flap of heavy flesh makes up a high forehead, suggesting an odd head-dress. Below the head and neck the body takes the appearance of a human being with well-defined chest and breasts. Like the stingray, it has a long pointed tail with spines along the entire length. On the tip end there are bands of heavy cartilage.

The under side of the fish was white whilst the upper side was sand-coloured. This suggests that, whatever it was, it may have foraged habitually on the ocean floor because such colouring would have been good camouflage for it. *(16)*

September, 1929

Thomas Bowen, a fisherman of Beach Haven, New Jersey, brought home a really strange one. It was just as well he got it home, he said, because nobody would have believed him otherwise.

The monster was caught in his net. It was too heavy for him to handle by himself so he called on four of his fishermen friends to help him. Even then, the five of them struggled for four hours before they managed to get it ashore.

It weighed 400 pounds and had wings which spread 9 feet, eyes in its ears, a 5-foot tail and two feet, each equipped with two toes. It was cream-coloured in front and royal purple on the back.   *(17)*

February, 1930

Another strange fish was caught at Waikiki in January, 1930. It had no tail, but it did have a combined mouth and nose, with only one tooth, a rudder and stabiliser similar to those on an aeroplane and was encased in a suit of armour.

This one is certainly not an unknown fish, although very rare. It is known to ichthyologists as *Raneania makua* and to the native Hawaiian as the apahu. It normally inhabits the extreme depths of the Pacific.   *(18)*

January, 1932

A fish monstrosity hanging outside a garage at Sea Cliff, Long Island, attracted a lot of attention from passing motorists and pedestrians. Its attraction was mainly in its ugliness and its enormous size.

It was 4 feet long, measured 27 inches across its back and weighed 110 pounds. Copper coloured, with an enormous mouth, three rows of teeth and a depressed head, it had fins which were rather like feet without legs. When opened, it was found to have swallowed, whole, 11 flounders.

The fish was found by Adolph Openhoskie in shallow water at a nearby beach. He killed it with a board to which a nail was attached. The strange fish was identified by local fishermen as an angler, a species which, they said, rarely comes into shallow water in those parts, except in cold weather. *(19)*

June, 1933

Another fish well-known to ichthyologists but certainly very strange in its life-style is the *photocorynus spiniceps*. Dr William K. Gregory, who was at the time the curator of fish at the American Museum of Natural History, gave the following description when his museum received a model of a live specimen:

> This species has developed parasitic males which, many times smaller than their relatively huge females, cling to the latter and in time become permanent and insignificant appendages of the females.
>
> In this odd design for living in the deep several males may be attached to one female, but in the model just received only one male is shown. As it happens, he hangs on for life above his "wife's" left eye, close to, but safe from, her cavernous mouth with its rows of needle-like teeth.
>
> Little is known about the species, but the theory has been advanced that the mature female throws out a powerful phosphorescent glow. The male comes rushing up and, in nine cases out of ten, disappears down her hungry jaws. The luckier males escape the trap and the snap of the great jaws by hanging onto the female's cheeks, throat, or, as in the case of the model, her left eye.
>
> The male's sharp little teeth then pierce the female's skin and he begins to feed upon the blood of his gigantic mate. As he hangs on with bulldog grip, the male is gradually transformed into a quasi-parasite and becomes attached to her for life. For that matter, the male is at no time able to support himself. He has no lure with which to bait fish and even if he had, his mouth is so small and his teeth so tiny that he could not feed himself. *(20)*

36

August, 1934

At St John's, Newfoundland, a giant fish was landed which was 26 feet long, 15 feet around the girth and with a tail 8 feet long. It had five rows of teeth, five sets of gills, five fins on its underbody and two on its back. *(21)*

August 1934

A fishing party that returned to Innisfail (Australia) reported that they had seen a sea monster between Mourilyan Harbour and Barnard Islands. They described it as being "nearly 50 feet in length and at least 8 feet across the back just below the head, which was shaped like that of a turtle, with small eyes and protruding teeth. There were large fins on the back and the tail appeared to be serrated and covered with large spikes."

The monster first appeared only 30 yards from their launch and they were able to get a good look at it as it swam slowly on the surface, its head several feet out of the water, gazing curiously at them. The strange creature stayed in the vicinity for 20 minutes. Then, for a short time it swam in circles, making a peculiar gasping, whistling sound, before heading out to sea. *(22)*

November, 1934

The year 1934 seems to have been a good one for sea monsters. Another one was reported in British Columbia. The remains were found on the beach near Porcher Island by Dr Neal Carter, director of the Dominion Fisheries Experimental Station at Prince Rupert.

It was 30 feet long and, although the flesh was decomposed, the creature appeared to have been a warm-blooded marine mammal with a head shaped something like that of a horse.

A few days later the Museum authorities at Victoria announced that the remains had been identified as those of a sea cow, native to Alaskan waters. *(23-24)*

December, 1934

A fish with four legs was caught by Mr B.O. Meyers in the Sugar River, near Beloit, Wisconsin. It was a kind of salamander, 20 inches long, with the head of a catfish and a long tail. *(25)*

March, 1935

The American Museum of Natural History was pleased to receive the first live specimens brought to the United States of an unusual species of fish which has four eyes. The fish are only small, about 3 inches long, but, amazingly, they can leap two feet out of the water. They are also able to swim backwards.

The fish were brought to the U.S. by Mr T. MacDougall, a naturalist. There were two pairs and they were caught by Mr MacDougall in their natural habitat in southern Mexico. The water had to be kept at 80 degrees F. or they would have died.

"Usually they swim along the surface of the water with their upper eyes out of the water and this unique system of vision makes them very difficult to catch," said Mr MacDougall. He added that from a strictly scientific viewpoint, "the four eyes should be regarded as two eyes, each having two pupils, because they are connected with each other internally". *(26)*

July, 1935

Two men fought with a sea monster two miles off Point Lonsdale, Victoria (Australia). Herbert and Arthur Hoppen were returning from a fishing cruise when they saw the creature heading straight for their boat.

Herbert Hoppen grabbed a rifle from his locker and fired at it, but missed. Then the monster tried to climb aboard their boat so Mr Hoppen reloaded the rifle and fired again. This time the bullet found its mark and the monster slid back into the sea and sank.

They described the creature as being about 20 feet long with a girth of 9 to 10 feet. Its head was large and shaped somewhat like a diver's helmet. Its eyes were as big as car headlights and it had a very long neck with black and white spots around it.   (27)

January, 1940

Transparent fish without eyes were found in water pumped from a well on an Ozark farm near Cureall, Montana. The owner of the farm said that the strange fish were discovered soon after the well was drilled. They were 2 to 5 inches long and resembled catfish. Their bones were clearly visible in the sunlight. They lived only a few hours after being brought to the surface, even though kept in water from the well. The well was 100 feet deep and the man who drilled it said the water came from an underground stream 6 feet deep.   (28)

January, 1948

The liner *Santa Clara* collided with, and apparently killed, a sea monster in the Caribbean Sea, off the coast of Columbia. The monster was seen clearly by three of the ship's officers and all three agreed on this description:

Its head was 3 feet across, 2 feet thick, and 5 feet long. It had a body 3 feet thick, a neck about 18 inches in diameter, and the visible part of its body was about 35 feet long.

The huge snake-like head of the serpent reared out of the sea only 30 feet off the starboard bow. The water about the ship was stained with blood and the officers believed that the liner cut the monster in two. The last they saw of it was when it was astern of the ship, threshing the water as though in its death agonies.   (29)

February 1949

A rare fish with a head like a cat and what looked like four legs, with paws, complete with claws, and with fur on its body was caught in a landing-net at Berowra Waters, New South Wales (Australia).

It was identified by Mr T.C. Roughley, Superintendent of

Fisheries, as a little known species of Angler fish, or *Antennarius striatus*. "It is very rare," he said, "and seldom seen because it does not go for a baited line. It crawls about the weeds in a river on its pectoral fins which are oddly shaped, bending forwards instead of backwards."

Mrs E. Withers, who caught the fish, said on the following day that she was keeping it alive, feeding it with prawns, just out of curiosity.

The fish was about 6 inches long, with tabby cat markings and whiskers. It even had shoulders and blew out behind itself in a form of jet propulsion.

The find caused tremendous interest among the local community. More than a thousand people came to look at it and at one stage caused a bad traffic jam. Eventually the fish was purchased for £25 by a country fish fancier. *(30-31)*

September, 1949

Mr and Mrs L. Keegan of Kyneton, Victoria (Australia) reported that several times in the previous fortnight they had seen a weird animal in the Laurisior Reservoir which adjoined their property. It was at least 4 feet in length, with long shaggy ears, but the amazing thing about it was that it used its ears to propel itself through the water "at tremendous speed".

"It dives and remains under water for a considerable distance before surfacing. When it submerges the noise can be heard from about 20 yards away," reported the Keegans.

Their story was supported by Mr J. Beare, a school teacher on holiday in the area, who had seen the animal twice and agreed with the description given by them. *(32)*

November, 1953

A two-headed barramundi was caught by Mr George Curran while he was fishing at the mouth of the Tully River in

Queensland (Australia). One head was on top of the other and each head appeared to be functioning normally, although the upper head was smaller than the lower one. The two heads merged into one body. *(33)*

November, 1960

The Australian mud skipper has a number of alternative names including kangaroo fish, climbing fish, Johnny jumper, etc. One of its odd characteristics is that it will die if kept submerged. Another is its ability to walk on land and even climb trees.

A fisherman once caught 30 or 40 of them and took them back to his hotel in a bucket. He placed the bucket in the laundry. Next morning he awoke to a chorus of screams from housemaids and waitresses. His fish had invaded various parts of the hotel and had even climbed the stairs! *(34)*

July, 1970

A tropical fish which lives among the coral reefs of the Red Sea, known scientifically as *Anthias squamipinnis*, is able to change sex on demand. Most of them grow up as females which, of course, gives the species a higher reproductive potential than they would have otherwise, but, if necessary, one or more of the females will change into males.

Dr Lev Fishelson of Tel-Aviv University proved this to be a fact by keeping groups of fish in tanks at the laboratory. If female fish are kept together without a male, one of them will gradually change sex after about two weeks. If this male is removed from the tank, another male will develop from the remaining females.

The mere sight of a male will prevent the females from changing sex. If the male is kept in the same tank but isolated by a glass screen, the females continue to be females.

When they are living their normal life in the sea, up to 90% of these fish are females. *(35)*

1982

A group of workers on a cattle station in North Queensland, Australia, once pulled off a very successful scientific hoax. They prepared a fake composite fish which comprised the body of a mullet, the tail of an eel and the bill of a platypus. Then they cooked their little monster and served it up to Mr Carl Staiger, the former director of the Brisbane Museum, for his evening meal.

Mr Staiger reacted exactly as the hoaxers had hoped. He was sucked in, hook, line and sinker, and forwarded a sketch and description of his unique find to a famous ichthyologist, Count Castelnan of France.

Count Castelnan named it *Ompax spatuloides* and it remained on the official list of Australian fishes from 1872 until 1930 when the hoax was discovered. *(36)*

September, 1983

A two-headed water snake became a star attraction at the Miami serpentarium during 1983, munching goldfish with gusto with each head. *(37)*

1983

In a book called *Living Wonders* two English authors, John Michell and Robert Rickard, suggest that Australia may be the home of the monster to out-monster all monsters – and it lives in the sea. They call it the "globster".

They claim that the globsters were first discovered on the west coast of Tasmania in 1960 when the body of one was washed up on a beach by a storm. A cattleman named Bill Fenton came across it.

The carcase measured 18 feet to 20 feet across. It was almost circular in shape and was covered by soft fur. It had a large mound in the centre and what appeared to be a set of gills.

Bruce Mollinson of the Commonwealth Scientific and Industrial Research Organisation, who examined it, said he had no idea what it was but hazarded a guess that it was a monstrous ray-like animal that lived deep in subterranean caverns off Tasmania.

The authors claim that other globster corpses have since been washed up on the Australian coast, some of them as big as houses.

A diver in the South Pacific is believed to be the only person to have seen a live globster. He described it as a great black mass, about an acre in extent, which rose up out of a chasm. The globster devoured a shark by "absorbing" it into its body.   *(38)*

Poisonous Fish

There are many fish in the Pacific Ocean which can be dangerous to eat if caught in particular localities, but are quite safe if caught elsewhere. There is, for example, the ulua of Hawaii which must never be taken on the channel side of Molokai, but if caught on the windward, or open ocean side, is quite harmless. It has been suggested that this effect is caused by the type of vegetation that the fish eat.   *(39)*

At Tahiti the haamea has a similar reputation, but is even more deadly. When caught in particular localities it causes severe inflammation and degeneration of the kidneys, which leads to death.

Another deadly fish which inhabits Tahitian waters is the nohu which has sharp spines along its back that are normally folded flat. It has a habit of burying itself in the sand in shallow water and if one steps on it, the spines automatically become erect so that they pierce the foot. Then it ejects a strong poison through the spines.   *(40)*

At Norfolk Island is found the strangest of these poisonous fish – the nanue, or "dream fish". It causes anyone who eats it to have violent nightmares. One fish expert, Mr T.C. Roughley, a former director of the New South Wales State Fisheries, said that for years he had refused to believe the stories about the dream fish. However, when he visited Norfolk Island he was forced to admit that they were true. He found that the stories were told by too many reliable people to be dismissed as nonsense. *(41)*

The Angler Fish

The angler fish is, as its name implies, an angler. He has a long narrow fin growing from his back which serves as a fishing rod and line. He bends this forward so that the tip is just in front of his mouth. Affixed to the tip is the "bait", a fleshy growth which looks like a worm and which the angler is able to wriggle very convincingly. When a smaller fish attempts to take the bait, he strikes. *(42)*

Mormyrids

In the rivers of central Africa there is a species of fish called mormyrids which "see" by means of electricity. The eyes of this fish are practically useless. With them, the fish can barely differentiate between light and darkness. And yet he is able to dart in and out between obstacles and pounce on small, quick fish.

He sends out a constant stream of small electrical discharges at the rate of about 300 per second and is able to sense any distortion in the electrical field caused by a nearby object.

Somehow, he is able to distinguish between living and non-living things, even when they are stationary. If two or more of these fish are operating in the same area, they change their frequency slightly so there is no confusion. *(43)*

The Epaulette Shark or "Ostrich Fish"

We all have probably heard at school the story of the ostrich burying its head in the sand and thinking that by doing so it could not be seen. I don't know about the ostrich but apparently there is a species of shark which shares that belief. It is the epaulette shark, a completely harmless variety which grows to a length of about 3 feet and has a tiny mouth and crushers instead of teeth. When anything happens to frighten this shark it rushes to the nearest rock and pushes its head under it, apparently unaware that the rest of its body remains in plain sight of its enemy. *(44)*

The Archer Fish

The archer fish of Southeast Asia shoots down its prey with a jet of water. Firing from beneath the surface of the water, it can hit insects up to three feet above the surface by squirting water up a tube formed between the palate and the tongue. *(45)*

The Coelacanth

The coelacanth is a strange fish, a real-life relic of prehistoric times. It disappeared from the fossil record 70 million years ago

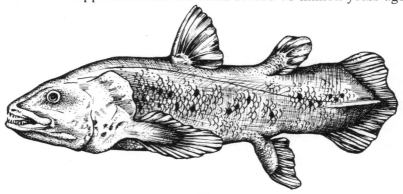

and was thought to be extinct until a live specimen was caught off the South African coast in 1938. The specimen was five feet long but, unfortunately, its value was not realised initially and it was only found possible to preserve the skeleton and the skin.

The fish was identified by Professor J.L.B. Smith of Rhodes University and the professor then began what turned out to be a long search for further specimens. He tramped up and down the eastern coast of Africa, talking to fishermen and distributing pamphlets in which he offered £100 for a specimen.

In December, 1952 a native fisherman caught a coelacanth in 65 feet of water just off the coast. Next morning he took it to the market but was prevented from selling it by an excited native who recognised it from Professor Smith's pamphlet and shouted, "Plenty money! Plenty money!"

When Professor Smith arrived to inspect the fish, he found it swathed in cotton wool and lying on the deck of a schooner. "I couldn't touch it," he said. "I asked them to open it." Then, when he saw it, he knelt down on the deck and wept. It was a coelacanth and, what was more, a different species from the 1938 specimen.

Since that time, about 200 further specimens have been caught near the Comoro Islands, off Madagascar.

The coelacanth (pronounced seal-a-kanth) usually lives on the ocean floor at a depth of about 1,000 to 2,000 feet. Most of the specimens that have been caught have been preserved and placed in museums throughout the world. However, the largest, which measures about 6 feet in length, is proudly displayed on the wall in the home of the President of the Comoro Islands.   (46-48)

The Octopus

The Pacific octopus is an amazing animal. It is the largest octopus in the world and has a spread of up to 32 feet with its tentacles outstretched. And yet, when it is first hatched, it is no larger than a grain of rice! During its early growth it increases in size by 20% each day.

The octopus likes to live out its two-to five-year existence in a dark underwater cave or crevice and its fastidious diet is shellfish – lobsters, crabs, oysters, etc. As far as possible, it stays in or close to home and usually only leaves its hide-out to mate.

Its locomotion is by jet propulsion. It sucks in water at the front and drives itself along by expelling the water behind it.

For protection, the octopus can camouflage itself by changing colour in an instant to blend in with its rocky background. It can also eject "ink" which provides a smoke-screen to hide it while it retreats to safety. If an enemy rips off a tentacle, the octopus simply grows another one.

It has a relatively large brain and this probably explains its cunning as a hunter. In one instance an octopus was observed to sit patiently alongside an oyster until it opened its shell. The octopus then placed a pebble so as to prevent the shell from closing and sucked out the occupant.

Despite its innate cunning, few octopuses live to maturity. The female normally lays up to 30,000 eggs, but only a handful survive to maturity.

The male leaves his lair to find a mate. Then, after they mate, he returns to his lair and dies. The female survives until her eggs hatch. Then she dies too. *(49)*

Wrasse

Tiny fish, called wrasse, regularly provide big fish like groupers with a teeth-cleaning service. The grouper opens its big mouth and rests quietly and patiently while the little fish swim around between his jaws, eating the bits of food stuck between his teeth. When the grouper feels his teeth are clean enough he slowly begins to close his jaws and the wrasse take this as a gentle hint that it is time for them to leave. *(50)*

5.   That's A Funny Way To Fish!

January, 1786

A hunter who had winged a duck and pursued it along the banks of the River Nene (U.K.), was still searching for his quarry when he was suddenly surprised to see an extremely large carp leap out of the water onto the bank about ten yards in front of him. He immediately shot it. Apparently the fish jumped out of the water in its last effort to escape the jaws of an otter which was a few yards behind and in close pursuit of it.   *(1)*

November, 1787

A number of men were lounging about the seashore near Happisburgh one Sunday in November, 1787 "instead of attending the important duties of the Sabbath", as *The Times* primly observed in the quaint fashion of newspapers in those days, when they saw a large cod-fish being rolled and battered against the rocks in shallow water nearby. It had been left stranded by the retreating tide and one of the men swore he would bring it ashore for his dinner-table.

He stripped off most of his clothes, plunged in and reached the fish without incident, then began to return to the shore, dragging the fish by the tail. He was thrown a rope by one of his companions but ignored it and shouted a vow "with horrid imprecations on himself" that he would bring the fish ashore on his own, as he had first proposed.

The report continued: "Scarcely had he uttered the words, when he fell, a lifeless corpse, his body floating on the water."   *(2)*

August, 1790

A party of ladies and gentlemen went fishing in a pond at East Bergholt, in Suffolk (U.K.), accompanied by a dog which, becoming thirsty, began lapping the water. Suddenly, a large jack lunged at the dog's tongue and bit it through. With a yelp, the dog swung his head back, and in doing so, tossed the jack up onto the bank where one of the company immediately grabbed hold of it. The fish was found to weigh more than 7 pounds. All of the party were greatly amused by the incident, with the exception of the dog who "was so much hurt, that he howled most bitterly for a considerable time after". *(3)*

January, 1818

The Chinese have invented a number of ingenious methods of fishing, most of which have been in use for centuries. In one, they make use of a flat board, painted white, and fixed on hinges to the side of the boat. In use, the board is inclined toward the water at an angle of about 45 degrees.

On moonlit nights the boat is placed so that the painted board is turned towards the moon. The rays of light from the moon strike the whitened surface and to the fish it appears to be moving water so they leap at it. At the right instant the fisherman pulls a cord attached to the board and flips them over into the boat. *(4)*

January, 1824

Another clever Chinese idea is one that is used in fish farming. The fishermen collect from the surface of the water the gelatine substance which contains fish spawn. They introduce this substance into a freshly-laid hen-egg that they have previously emptied, stop up the hole and place the egg under a sitting hen. After a specific number of days they break the shell into water that has been warmed by the sun. The young fish then hatch and are kept in the water until they are big enough to be thrown into one of the breeding ponds with older fish. *(5)*

May, 1829

The Oriental Herald (Calcutta) of May 24, 1829 published an eye-witness report of an extraordinary fight between an Indian, who was armed only with a rope, and a large shark. The witness, an Englishman, said that he noticed a commotion among all the people at the water's edge and, on investigating, found that it had been caused by the appearance of a large shark close to the shore. The shark was apparently pursuing a fish among the boats that were moored there.

Our witness then observed a native holding a rope, which he had tied into a kind of running knot, and manoeuvring his boat after the shark with the evident intention of lassoing it. When next the shark came to the surface, about six or eight yards from the boat, the native plunged into the water and boldly swam towards it.

The shark turned and swam slowly and, it seemed, warily towards its human opponent. When the antagonists were only a foot or two from each other, the man dived suddenly below the shark and, seconds later, reappeared on the other side of his quarry. During these contortions, the native was swimming, using only one hand, the other being behind his back holding the rope.

They came together again, and this time the shark raised itself over the lower part of the native's body in an attempt to seize him with its teeth. But, at this instant, displaying great speed and strength, the native threw himself up out of the water, then plunged down feet foremost, "the shark following him so simultaneously, that I was fully impressed with the idea that they had gone down grappling together. As far as I could judge, they remained nearly 20 seconds out of sight, while I stood in breathless anxiety, and, I may add, horror, waiting the result of this fearful encounter. Suddenly the native made his appearance, holding up both of his hands over his head, and calling out with a voice that proclaimed the victory he had won while underneath the water, 'Tan-tan!' "

The man's companions in the boat were all prepared. They dragged the monster ashore despite its fierce struggles and killed it. The shark was measured and found to be almost 7 feet long.

The hero of this exploit suffered only a cut on his left arm from coming into contact with the shark's tail or fins.

Said the witness, "It did not occur to me to ask if this was the first shark-fight in which he had been engaged; but from the preparations and ready assistance he received from his companions in the boats, I should suppose that he has more than once displayed the same courage and dexterity which so much astonished me. The scene was altogether one I shall never forget." *(6)*

December, 1841

The legendary ferocity of the pike was demonstrated once again after a flood in the United Kingdom, on the River Leam. A group of boys were paddling in the retreating floodwaters when the foot of one of them was seized by a pike which weighed about 4 pounds. It was only after a fierce battle that the boy managed to disengage the fish from his foot, following which, nursing his wounds, he carried it home to his delighted family for an enjoyable meal. *(7)*

March, 1845

An unusual discovery was made during routine maintenance at a wharf in the United Kingdom. An anchor was hauled up and the workmen were surprised to see movement inside a hole in the stock of this piece of equipment. After driving off the hoops and taking the stock apart, they found that the tenant was a black conger eel, about 4 feet long and weighing more than 10 pounds. He had obviously entered this abode when very young because the hole on the outside was not large enough to admit a creature half his size. He was too large to turn around in the space he had available, but somehow he must have found sufficient food, not only to live, but to live well, for he was a fine, fat specimen. *(8)*

June, 1848

Workmen collecting gravel on the River Trent (U.K.), had a stroke of luck when they were able to grab hold of an 18-pound salmon which, for some reason, leaped into their boat. *(9)*

July, 1853

James Burnett, a night-watchman at the works and foundry near the South Wales railway bridge at Chepstow (U.K.), was surprised early one morning to hear unusual sounds coming from the river. His bulldog, which was accompanying him on his rounds, plunged into the water to investigate. After a tremendous struggle, the dog was successful in bringing to shore the source of all the noise – a large ling fish. This species was rarely found in the River Wye and this particular specimen proved to be a very large one – no less than 15 pounds. *(10)*

July, 1897

A dog in another part of the world some decades later was somewhat less successful in his encounter with a member of the finny tribe. Three small boys in Narrowsburg, on the Delaware River, New York State, decided to teach their jointly-owned pug dog how to swim. *The New York Times* reporter who wrote the story about the events that followed apparently had a very low opinion of this particular breed of dog. One of his opening remarks was that "it is a well-known zoological fact that all dogs except pugs soon learn to swim, but pugs have never been known to learn anything". He went on to say that, taking this into account, and considering the fact that the boys were determined and the water was deep, it was a fair bet that this dog was going to get drowned.

The method the boys chose to teach their dog to swim was the plain and simple one of tying a cord around his neck and throwing him over the stern of the boat. A continuous yelping from the dog eventually convinced the boys that there could be some reason for his complaints, apart from his dislike of the water, so they hauled him back on board again.

They discovered that their suspicions were correct. Still fiercely attached to the pug's body was a 24-pound catfish. *(11)*

July, 1924

Joseph Hand, of Cape May, during a period of ten days in July, 1924, broke all hand-line fishing records on the New Jersey coast. His nick-name was "Harbour Pike". While fishing in Cold Springs inlet, he caught more than 1,000 pounds of weakfish. "Harbour Pike" apparently had some secret method which gave him a tremendous advantage over other fishermen. A syndicate offered him a large sum to divulge the secret but he declined. It was generally believed that the secret was the bait that he used. Whatever it was, fish rose to Hand's line continually while other fishermen who were fishing nearby could not even get a nibble. The most "Harbour Pike" would say about his secret was that it was something that had been told to him by an old Indian Chief who had passed through the city some time previously with a medicine company. *(12)*

September, 1926

For centuries the Chinese and Japanese have used specially-trained cormorants to catch fish. One Japanese emperor went fishing, using this method, hundreds of years ago and, so

delighted was he with his deliciously-flavoured trout, that he wrote a poem in honour of the occasion. The poem is preserved in the *Kojiki*, the Record of Ancient Matters.

A man who visited Japan in 1926 was fascinated by this unusual fishing method, and this is his story of how it was carried on at that time. In some places, at least in China, the method is still in use today.

The cormorants that were used for this purpose were island-cormorants, a particular species that will not breed in captivity. They were caught very young and two seasons were spent in training them. A season lasted from May to October. Fishing was done every night, except when there was a full moon.

The fishing was done on the Nagara River, the boats being allowed to drift downstream with the current. On each boat was an iron basket full of blazing faggots. Fish were drawn to the boats by the light from the fires and they fell easy prey to the big, black birds.

Each of the birds had a ring made of fibre or whalebone around its throat. The size of the ring was such that the bird was prevented from swallowing large fish; however, he was able to swallow small fish for his own supper. Each bird was also tethered by a 12-foot line to prevent his escape.

The birds were lowered to the water where they would dart about busily catching fish. Each time a bird caught a fish, his handler would lift him from the water, squeeze his throat to force him to drop the catch, then lower him to the water again.

The birds had a fierce pecking order. An old bird was No. 1 bird – the big boss. His place was at the bow of the boat and he had to be last to be put in the water and first to be taken out. The other birds had their specific order and there was a terrible commotion if that order was broken.

During the winter, the birds lived inside the fishermens' huts and they were very well looked after, as one would expect, because they were regarded as being very valuable. *(13)*

October, 1928

A group of men playing cards in the saloon of the *Eleanor Bolling*, supply ship of the Byrd Antarctic expedition, were surprised when a flying fish came in through a porthole and interrupted their game. It hit one player on the shoulder, then bounced onto the table, scattering their cards.

The saloon was situated about the centre of the vessel and the porthole through which the fish entered was 10 feet above the waterline.

The fish was a fine specimen, about 11 inches long, and was served for breakfast on the following morning. *(14)*

September, 1931

Indians in the Turrialba district of Costa Rica fish with bows and arrows. They will stand in water up to their waists for hours waiting for their prey.

Another of their methods is to use a shrub they call *barbasco* which has a powerful poison in its leaves. First, they erect a cane fence across a stream; then they throw the plant into the water about half-a-mile upstream. The poison from the plant causes fish to become blinded and disorientated and they float on the surface down to the cane barrier where they are easily scooped out of the water.

In Ethiopia, two fish poisons are used. One comes from the seeds of the barberra tree. The seeds are ground up into a powder which is sprinkled onto the surface of the water in dry seasons when the stream is flowing sluggishly.

In Malaysia, the tuba root is used in a similar fashion. By rubbing the roots together, a toxic secretion is produced which renders the fish unconscious. Meanwhile, a crowd of Malays waits further down where the stream widens out into shallow water and the fish can be easily caught. *(15)*

January, 1932

Constable Bresnan, gatekeeper at Government House, Canberra (Australia), did some unusual fishing one day to solve a wildlife problem.

He slept in a cubicle at the main gates to the building and began to hear strange noises during the night coming from under the floor. He assumed it was rats, so set a trap near a hole in the foot of the outside wall, but with no result. Then he spotted a brown snake disappearing down the hole.

He caught a frog, affixed it to a fish hook on the end of a strong line, and tied the other end of the line to a stake. Then he dropped the bait down the hole. Not long afterwards he saw the line tighten. He pulled the line and hauled out a struggling brown snake which he despatched by breaking its back with a stick. The snake was 4 feet 6 inches long. It had swallowed the frog and the hook had pierced its throat about 3 inches below the mouth. *(16)*

January, 1933

A member of the Chicago Museum's zoological staff, Mr Karl P. Schmidt, writing in *The Field Museum News,* reported that he had learnt about a new way to fish during a visit to San Salvador. He had watched an Indian girl use the method with considerable success.

She would walk in the water at low tide, pick up small rocks and hurl them with all her might against large rocks under which fish customarily hide. The concussion from the impact stunned the fish and enabled her to catch them. *(17)*

January, 1933

When three sharks got into the swimming pool at Sandgate Pier, Queensland (Australia), Mr Roy Wilson decided to use rodeo tactics to get rid of them. He leaped on the back of one of them, hooked his legs around its body and held tight. The shark dashed up and down the pool repeatedly but was not able to dislodge Mr Wilson. It finally stopped, exhausted and beaten, and was captured and dragged out of the pool. Mr Wilson then repeated his performance with each of the other two sharks.

The sharks were of the shovel-nosed variety and ranged from 6 to 9 feet in length. According to Mr Wilson, this species of shark is not dangerous unless cornered. *(18)*

February, 1933

A big one was not allowed to get away by Mr T. Moynihan, of Nangus (Australia), when he was fishing in the Murrumbidgee River. He had a 35-pound fish hooked but it was on a light line which he feared would break before he got the fish ashore. Handing the line to his friend, Mr Moynihan jumped into the water and struggled to shore with the fish in his arms. *(19)*

June, 1935

Fishing was easy near Canadian, Texas, on June 20, 1935. In fact, people fished with their bare hands. Fish up to 10 pounds in weight were picked up on the ground by the thousand after a cloudburst destroyed a number of dams on a nearby lake system.[20]

July, 1935

Two men at Halifax, Nova Scotia, struck a big fish which seemed determined to get caught. Frank Gilroy and Martin Moore had no fishing gear with them when they saw the fish swimming in shallow water. They poked a stick towards it and the fish grabbed the stick between its teeth and held on grimly while they hauled it up onto the bank.

It was 5 feet long, weighed 75 pounds, had a head 2 feet wide, flippers on each side, two rows of small, sharp teeth and, projecting from its underbody, two things that looked like hands.

It was thought to be a monkfish or an angler. *(21)*

October, 1935

Captain New and his crew of the ferry boat *Paunpeck*, had a most unusual experience when they were crossing the Hudson River. It suddenly began to rain eels. One landed on the roof of the pilot house and bounced off onto the deck. Then another eel landed on the deck alongside it.

The men looked at each other in amazement for a moment. Then, deckhand Joseph Neves provided a logical, down-to-earth explanation for the strange occurrence. Two seagulls had been foraging for food and each had scored an eel. They were flying across the river, each with an eel in its mouth, and happened to be directly above the ferry when Captain New sounded a shrill blast on his siren. This frightened the daylights out of the birds, so much so that they dropped the eels out of their mouths. *(22)*

December, 1935

Flying fish have always been one of the staple items in the diet of the inhabitants of Barbados, an island in the West Indies. Hundreds of boats are engaged in fishing for them, each with a crew of two or three men. The fish live in schools which number thousands and they usually grow to about a foot in length.

The boats are painted blue to camouflage them on the blue, tropic water and the fishermen maintain absolute silence. They catch the flying fish in nets.

Studies by zoologists have shown that the fish do not actually fly. They glide. Their fins are used to stabilise them in flight. Propelled by their powerful tails, they leap into the air and, as far as possible, use the air currents above the uneven surface of the water to keep them aloft.

Usually, flying fish glide close to the surface of the ocean so that they can extend their flight by a flick of the tail against the water. However, they have been observed to rise to a height of 20 feet in the air and to glide as far as 1,300 feet. Their gliding speed is normally up to about 20 mph. *(23-24)*

August, 1936

All sorts of excitement ensued when Billy Ray, of Long Island, decided to take his pet monkey, Chico, with him when he went fishing. He set out, with two friends, in a rowing boat and the fishing spot they had selected was reached without incident. The three humans then settled down to some quiet fishing.

Chico was restless though and hopped about the boat chattering incessantly. Billy Ray gave the monkey a fishing line to play with in an effort to quieten her down. Imitating the humans, Chico pulled up the line and, sure enough, on the hook was a weakfish.

The fish was taken aboard and Billy was detaching it from the hook when suddenly the craft was rocked by pandemonium. Chico began bounding about the boat screeching at full volume. It turned out that her tail, which she had let trail in the water, had been attacked by a large crab and the crab was still holding onto the appendage stubbornly.

When the party returned to shore Chico, despite her still-sore tail, was obviously proud of herself as she displayed her two trophies, the weakfish and the crab. *(25)*

September, 1936

A Canadian fisherman, Hedley McCluskey, of Fredericton, was playing an 11-pound salmon when it jumped into his canoe in an effort to hurdle the craft. McCluskey ended the contest by hitting the fish with his paddle.
(26)

April, 1937

At Warragul, Victoria (Australia), workmen employed by the State Rivers and Water Supply Commission were engaged in de-snagging the Latrobe River when they winched ashore a huge, hollow log. In the middle of it they found an English trout which weighed more than 5 pounds.
(27)

May, 1937

On May 1, 1937, the day the pickerel season opened on Silver Lake, Alex Judson of Perry, New York, was lucky enough to catch a fine specimen with a beer bottle. He had suspended the bottle in the water to keep it cool but, a short time later, he noticed a jerking on the cord. "I pulled in the line," he said, "and there was the pickerel, caught on a tooth of the metal cap."
(28)

May, 1937

Harold Gardener, of Albany, was fishing in the Hudson River when he caught a 15-pound northern pike by pulling up his anchor. The fish had been hooked and in its struggles it wound the line round and round until it eventually managed to tie itself securely to the anchor.
(29)

June, 1937

A trout was once caught by a train en route to Chicago. When the *City of Denver* arrived at its destination on June 7, 1937, it was found that the headlight was broken and, inside it, was a dead trout. The explanation was that, whilst the train was travelling at 80 mph, an eagle had swooped into its path. And, of course, the eagle had been carrying the trout.
(30)

June, 1937

In the same month, another fish fell victim to an automobile. Richard Root, of New York, was the witness. "A sucker worked its way up over a fordway in Enfield Creek, when along came a roadster," he explained. "The roadster struck the water and threw up a big splash – and the fish. The driver stopped the car, got out, and took the fish away." *(31)*

June, 1937

William F. O'Day, a chauffeur, successfully fished in a street in Buffalo, New York. Many streets in the city had been flooded by heavy rain and he thought he would try his luck. In fashionable Nottingham Terrace he caught a 14-inch sucker. *(32)*

June, 1937

Another fish was caught under unusual circumstances in Buffalo during the same month when it rose up out of the depths of Lake Erie to snap at the propeller of an outboard motor.

William L. Kirst and Albert Wild were trolling for pike when their copper line got caught up in the boat's propeller. They tilted the engine up to unsnarl the line. A 12-pound sturgeon, down in the depths of the lake, evidently looked up, saw the shining blades of the propeller and mistook them for fish. It came flying up at full speed, missed its target, sailed clear out of the water and landed in William Kirst's lap. After a struggle, as it thrashed about in the boat, they managed to subdue it.

"That's it," said Kirst. "Here's the fish, without a hook mark on him, and now you can bring on your lie detector." *(33)*

July, 1937

During the following month another fish was caught at Hamilton, Bermuda, when it made a somewhat similar mistake. Pilot Augustus Minors lit his cigarette and threw the empty packet into St George's Harbour. A fish 18 inches long mistook the packet for a morsel of food. It came rushing up from the deep water, overshot the mark, and landed on the dock at Minor's feet. The pilot happily took it home for dinner. *(34)*

July, 1937

Also at Bermuda, and in the same month, another unusual catch was made by Terry Mowbray, sports director of the Bermuda Trade Development Board, and Miss Priscilla Hollister, of Corning, New York. The couple were cruising around Harrington Sound in a small outboard motor boat when they saw a large rockfish swimming close to the surface. Both were keen on fishing but on this particular occasion they were in the frustrating position of having no fishing gear aboard. They decided to follow it, regardless, and their chase was rewarded. After about an hour, Mowbray managed to stab the fish with a screwdriver. His companion rammed the boat's small anchor down its throat and together they dragged the fish aboard. *(35)*

August, 1937

An aborigine named Charlie fought and beat a 6-foot crocodile in the King River, near Wyndham, in Western Australia. Charlie had been walking alongside the river bank with the intention of catching a baby crocodile for food. He saw one that he thought was about 3 feet long and went into the water after it. But the water was muddy. Charlie was mistaken. The crocodile was not a baby. It was half-grown.

Charlie only realised his error after he had dived under the crocodile and seized it around the body. The fight lasted for 10 minutes before Charlie was able to throw it up onto the bank. The struggle then continued there for several more minutes. Eventually, Charlie was the victor. He used strips of stringy bark to tie up the crocodile's jaws and lash its back legs to its tail. He then carried it to a pumping station on the river where it was skinned.

Charlie suffered badly lacerated hands. *(36)*

January, 1938

Frankie Tate, a five-year-old boy, of Westerly, Rhode Island, had a fish story to tell after catching his first fish. Frankie had been skating on Blackbird Pond when he cut a hole in the ice and then decided to poke his finger into the water to test the temperature. He pulled his finger out faster than he put it in. Firmly attached to the forefinger was an 8-inch pickerel. *(37)*

April, 1938

A floppy-eared cocker spaniel named Sonny demonstrated a new way to fish when he drank from a trough. While the dog was drinking, a 16-inch, 2-pound trout, which had been living in the trough for the previous two years, sank its teeth into one of Sonny's dangling ears. The dog jerked his head back in fright, and, in doing so, tossed the fish 10 feet away.

Sonny's owner said that even though it was April Fool's Day, the dog didn't think it was much of a joke at all. *(38)*

May, 1938

Some cunning motorists in Georgia were reported to be using what was apparently an effective, although strictly illegal, method of fishing. They were running a wire from one of the spark plug leads and letting the other end of the wire dangle in the water. They would then speed up the motor so as to generate an electric current strong enough to stun fish that came near the wire into insensibility.

A local official, Warden Lennox Henderson, threatened that any motorist caught using this method would get as much of a shock as the fish when he received his fine. *(39)*

May, 1939

Jim Stoker, of Albemarle, North Carolina, claimed that when he went fishing he didn't need to take any fancy fishing tackle. His dog would dive in and bring fish to the bank for him. *(40)*

July, 1941

Another man who did not need fishing tackle was Macon Henry, of Hickory, North Carolina. He went fishing one day; then discovered that he had forgotten to bring any fish hooks. He thought he would have a swim instead and plunged into the Catawba River. He caught his foot in a large pickle jar lying on the bottom of the stream, brought it ashore and found inside it two catfish, each about 9 inches long. *(41)*

August, 1941

George Slick and his son-in-law, Joseph Stetzel, went fishing and used an 18-inch sashweight to anchor their boat. A pike weighing 14 pounds 11 ounces gobbled up the sashweight as soon as they dropped it overboard. He was quickly hauled on board. Inside him they found a 3-pound bass. *(42)*

March, 1942

A war dispatch from Port Moresby on March 25, 1942 stated that troops stationed there would have fresh fish for supper that night, courtesy of the Japanese Air Force. There had been an air raid during the day but the only casualties were thousands of fish stunned by the bombs exploding in the harbour. As soon as the Jap planes disappeared, boats swarmed out to scoop up the fish floating on the surface. *(43)*

July, 1943

Another fish story from World War II was reported on July 19, 1943 when a British Empire Medal was awarded to ship's carpenter, T.W. Chapman of South Shields. Chapman used his hand as bait for the capture of a 5-foot shark to feed a boatload of seamen whose ship had been torpedoed.

The men had been drifting in an open boat for 22 days and were weakening from lack of food. Chapman placed his hand in the water and waited for the shark to lunge at it. He then grabbed the shark by the gills, wrestled it on board and killed it. *(44)*

July, 1945

When the crew of the freighter *Amhearst Victory* pulled up anchor in the Mississippi, they accidentally hooked an enormous fish that did not get away. The anchor appeared to foul something as it was being drawn up, then it came clear out of the water with a 4-ton fish attached.

Dr James N. Gowanloch, chief biologist of the Louisiana Department of Fisheries, identified it as a two-horned manta. It was 18 feet square and weighed 8,000 pounds. *(45)*

February 1946

It was reported that workmen in Madrid had caught a trout weighing 4 pounds merely by opening a water-pipe in one of the city streets. They had it for dinner that night but they suspected no one really believed their story about where it came from. *(46)*

June, 1946

Some species in the fish kingdom could be termed "hitch-hikers", one such being the shark sucker. He can swim, but he prefers to ride and, for this purpose, has developed a powerful sucking disc on his head. He uses this to attach himself to the underside of a large fish.

Natives in some parts of the Pacific use the shark sucker to catch fish. They tie a rope to his tail, throw him into the water and, when he has attached himself to a large fish, haul them both in. A shark sucker has been used in this fashion to catch a fish weighing 24 pounds. *(47)*

March, 1947

An Australian at Concord railway-station, Sydney, could hardly believe his eyes when he turned on a water tap and saw a fish 6 inches long and three-quarters of an inch thick emerge.

Water Board officials said that fish eggs sometimes got into the pipes and hatched there.

The fish was later identified as a Murray cod. *(48)*

October, 1947

In Iceland, near a place called Laugar, there is a spot where it is possible to land a fish already cooked. First, you catch a trout in an icy-cold mountain stream; then you swing it over and drop it into the boiling water of a nearby hot spring. Finally, you drop it onto the picnic table. *(49)*

April, 1948

A story was reported about Sam, a man who liked to do everything the easy way, even fishing. And, one day he found the perfect answer – at least, so far as fishing was concerned.

When the reporter came across Sam he had a large fish in his basket, which, he said, he had caught in the easiest possible way.

Before this master stroke, however, he admitted that he had been fishing unsuccessfully for some time. Then he sat down and watched a fish-hawk at work. After circling around for a while, the bird swooped down to the water and came up with a salmon. Then he headed back toward his nest. When the bird was directly overhead, Sam clapped his hands together hard. The bird got such a fright that he dropped his burden and, believe it or not, it fell right into Sam's basket. *(50)*

September, 1948

Natives in the Trobriand Islands, Papua, shoot prawns with a palm leaf arrow. They are made from palm leaf splinters cut as thin and sharp as needles. *(51)*

March, 1950

Mr G.W. Smith of Sydney (Australia) has pioneered a new method of fishing which he said had been very successful. He flew kites from the top of Ben Buckler, a high cliff at Bondi, to carry his fishing lines out over the water.

Mr Smith said, "By flying out my line I can get out over 300 yards from the cliffs. I can fly out over the heads of other fishermen on the rocks below."

The line ran through a small pulley below the kite. Mr Smith caught six fish the first time he tried this method, two of which were more than 3 pounds each. *(52)*

April, 1950

Resourcefulness paid off for Mr C.U. McDonald, of the State of Washington, when he arrived at his favourite fishing spot and discovered he had left his hooks at home. He spotted a bright new can-opener among his gear, tied it to a line and caught 16 silver trout. *(53)*

April, 1950

A short, sharp contest took place between Robert Golding and an eagle for possession of a 2-pound salmon that was dropped out of the sky. The fish was dropped on Mr Golding's farm by a fish hawk but an eagle swooped down with the intention of picking it up. Mr Golding beat the eagle to it and frightened the bird off by waving a stick at it. *(54)*

April, 1951

Crocodiles apparently like music. A crocodile-hunting party at Darwin (Australia) discovered this when they took a portable gramophone with them on a hunting expedition.

As the music floated out over the water, three crocodiles nosed in close to the pier to listen. For one croc, the interest in music proved fatal.

A member of the party said, "The crocodiles were obviously fascinated by the music. Now that the crocodile shooting season is starting again, that gramophone and a dozen records will become an essential part of our gear. We'll try and find out what music they like best, though it seems to me they appreciate anything from boogie to Bach." (55)

November, 1951

A 5-foot shark caused some excitement when it got into the public swimming pool at Sandringham, Sydney (Australia).

Two 13-year-old boys floated out on a tyre to do battle with the intruder, using an iron spike. They hit it several times. Later, they went out again armed with a crow bar but were not able to find the shark.

Residents said that the shark must have got into the pool at high tide. (56)

February, 1952

At Queensland University (Australia) Professor W. Stephenson reported that he was engaged in teaching fish to take a baited line. He used special soft hooks which straightened out when the fish swallowed them so that the fish would survive and enable him to carry on with his experiments.

He was working with golden perch and soon had the fish trained so that they would swallow a bait as soon as it was thrown to them. The main purpose of the experiments was to gain information on their food preferences. Preliminary indications from the research were that the fish seemed to have a decided preference for fresh-water prawns. (57)

June, 1953

Hundreds of fresh fish were found among trees and bushes on the hills at La Conrera, near Barcelona, after a violent storm and hurricane on the coast five miles away. Campers gathered them and cooked them for lunch. (58)

July, 1953

A great shoal of tuna in Darwin Harbour provided residents with the best fishing they had enjoyed for many years. Tuna rarely come into the harbour but this time they apparently followed a school of sardines. The fish were so abundant that small boys were flipping them out onto the shore by their tails. Some of the fish weighed as much as 5 pounds. *(59)*

January, 1957

Peter Button, aged 18, of Coffs Harbour, New South Wales (Australia), secured his catch, a 7-foot 6-inch shark, by jumping on its back and attaching a rope to it.

He caught the shark from the jetty and played it from there for some time. Then, he jumped onto the beach and attempted to drag it ashore. As he was hauling it in the shark broke free so Button rushed into the surf, jumped on its back and slipped a noose over its tail. He then landed the shark, which weighed 179 pounds. *(60)*

Golfing Fishermen

I came across three separate instances during my research where a fish was bagged by a golfer:

In February, 1937 James Sinclair was playing at the Miami Biltmore golf course when he half-topped a shot on the 7th hole. The ball sped towards a creek. A cavorting mullet was the fish that was in the wrong place at the wrong time. He popped his head up and was struck by the ball near the gills and killed instantly. *(61)*

Jupe Wallin was playing on his local golf course at Ashland, Oregon, in April, 1939 when he hooked the ball into an irrigation ditch. It hit, and stunned, a 20-inch, 6-pound trout which Wallin took home for dinner. *(62)*

In May, 1957 a golfer sliced his shot into a lake at the 18th hole at Killarney, Eire. A trout was the unfortunate fish who chose that moment to swallow an insect above the surface. He floundered about near the surface in a dazed condition until two fishermen waded in and brought him ashore. They also retrieved the golf ball. *(63)*

Incidentally, it is not only fish that have to worry about golfers. A fat, unsuspecting mountain duck in full flight was brought down by a golfer at Perth, Australia, in July, 1957. Warren Smith was playing a social game on the municipal links at Wembley, a few miles from Perth, when he played a wood shot on the 13th fairway. Smith was surprised when his ball brought down an even more surprised mountain duck. He took the duck home for dinner even though it had not been acquired in the approved manner. *(64)*

August, 1958

A rowing race was about to begin at the Westcliff Regatta at Herne Bay (U.K.) when a bass weighing over 3 pounds leaped into the Herne Bay Amateur Rowing Club junior four's boat.

The coxswain, D. Browning, said, "Suddenly there was a flash and something came over the shoulder of stroke. There was a thud in the boat and when I looked down a big fish was flapping on the floor boards." The crew finished second and when they crossed the line the bass was still flapping at their feet. The club members had it for dinner that night. *(65)*

August, 1959

Mr Frederick Allen, manager of a hotel at Mousehole, Cornwall (U.K.), whilst preparing for bed, took advantage of the strategic location of his bedroom by throwing a fishing line out of the window. He caught a 5-pound mullet, believed to be the first mullet caught in the harbour for years. *(66)*

November, 1962

A dog named Major built quite a reputation for himself in his part of the United Kingdom during the 1960's for his ability at glatting – hunting conger eels.

All his owner had to do was follow Major as he sniffed around rocks uncovered by the receding tide and lever up the rocks indicated by the dog. When he sniffed an eel, Major would stand still quivering until the rock was rolled over. *(67)*

Bare-handed Fishing

Over the years there have been some impressive feats in bare-handed fishing. For example, Mr O. A. Gane, a real estate dealer, from West Palm Beach, Florida, was fishing for pompano in April, 1936 when he saw a large fin close to the shore. He jumped into the water, grabbed the fish by the tail and hauled it ashore. It proved to be a 9-foot 8-inch blue marlin sword fish which weighed 149 pounds. *(68)*

At Beach Haven, New Jersey, not long after, a man with the appropriate name of George Rambo, ran into the sea and dragged out a 19-pound tuna. *(69)*

At Caister, Norfolk (U.K.), in February, 1962, a woman, Mrs Eileen Bond, aged 51, saw a 34-pound cod in the breakers. She grabbed it and pulled it onto the beach. *(70)*

In September, 1958 a young mother, Mrs Mayne Maceira, was paddling in shallow water with her two small children, aged 2 and 3, on the beach at Monteray, California, when she saw a shark in the surf. Mrs Maceira first got her children to safety, then went after the 7-foot blue shark and grabbed it by the tail. Twice, she lost her footing as she struggled with it but eventually she managed to drag it ashore. Then she beat it to death with a nail-studded board! *(71)*

June, 1967

Motorists at King's Lynn, Norfolk (U.K.), were astounded when they saw a man, who looked reasonably sane, fishing with rod and line in a hole that had been dug in the road by workmen. The man was Gus Routledge. What the motorists did not know, however, and what Mr Routledge did know, was that a sewer fed by the tide ran directly underneath that spot. Mr Routledge was fishing for conger eels and he had a very successful day. He and a friend caught 45 pounds of eels. *(72)*

1969

The proprietor of a fishing lodge at Taupo, New Zealand, told the story of one of his guests who had a most unusual attitude towards his favourite sport of fishing. He was an American, Dr Pierce, from New York.

The doctor found it boring to wade into the river, cast his line and stand there waiting, and waiting, for a fish to bite. So, he regularly paid a local Maori to take over that irksome task for him.

Dr Pierce would find a comfortable spot on the bank of the stream and settle down to read a book. When a trout took the bait he would put a bookmark between the pages, take over the rod, and play the trout.

"I can't be bothered wasting time casting," he would say, "It's the fun of fighting them I like." *(73)*

1982

David Palmer, 17, a member of the relieving staff of a bank, was doing a stint at the Mount Isa branch in Queensland (Australia). After work one day, he went for a swim in Lake Moondarra and during the swim he cut his foot.

The foot was painful during the next couple of days. It swelled, and a large blister formed. Palmer returned to Brisbane, where he saw his doctor who opened the blister – and out popped a live half-inch fish!

The fish apparently entered the wound, was trapped inside when the wound sealed over and continued to live in the liquid within the blister. *(74)*

Rick Palmer, from near Narrandera, N.S.W. (Australia), was retrieving cattle from a flooded gully when he spotted a big Murray cod in the water. Using his horse in round-up fashion he forced the cod into shallow water, then leaped onto it and dragged it ashore. The cod weighed 45 pounds. *(75)*

At Coffs Harbour, N.S.W. (Australia), a man was eating oysters from the piles under the bridge when he accidentally dropped one into the water. Instantly, a 15-pound jewfish appeared, ready to snap it up but, just as quickly, the man's dog grabbed the jewfish by the tail and dragged it onto the bank. *(76)*

Mr Hector Cracknell, of Nundah (Australia), discovered that his dog's particular gift was finding and bailing up mud crabs which Mr Cracknell would happily gather up and pop into a bag. *(77)*

The Fijians use a very clever method to catch coconut crabs. When he knows one of the crabs has climbed a tree, the Fijian ties a ring of turf around the trunk of the tree about 10 feet from the ground. The crab descends the trunk backwards. When he feels the turf with his back feet he thinks he has reached ground level so he lets go, tumbles off and is killed in the fall. *(78)*

1987

In his book *Reflections from the Water's Edge*, British angler, John Bailey, shared with his readers the story of an ingenious experiment he carried out, which was aimed at attracting fish to his bait.

Bailey had been fishing successfully for perch in a reservoir and the thing about this particular fishing-hole that impressed him was the clearness of the water. The fish "grew large on rich food supplies and the clarity of the water gave them a brilliance of colour and marking I found mind-blowing.

"I had bought a large, thick-walled goldfish bowl and I whittled a huge cork slab to fit it tightly. I filled the bowl, the size of a football, with water and put in it about 20 sticklebacks and gudgeon. In went the cork stopper and, attaching the bowl to a rope, I threw it in.

"My idea was that the bowl would act as a type of attractor, or groundbait. It worked! In the clear water of the reservoir, you could see the perch gather around it and peer at the captives inside as though they were watching a submerged TV set. I swear you could hear them lick their lips on hungry days and a bait dropped nearby would be snaffled at once." *(79)*

6. And When I Cut It Open ...

December, 1787.

Early in December, 1787 some fishermen who were using nets in the Thames, near Poplar, found, to their surprise, that they had captured a large shark. The report in *The Times* did not give the length but stated that it was the largest fish of the species ever seen by any person in the Thames.

It was only with great difficulty that they got it into their boat. The shark was still alive, but in a dying state.

What made this catch even more remarkable was what was found when they cut it open. There was a silver watch, a metal chain and a Cornelian seal, together with several pieces of gold lace. The watch had the name of Henry Watson, London, No. 1369 and the works were said to be much impaired.

It was surmised that a wealthy, young gentleman had somehow fallen victim to the monster, perhaps by falling overboard, and that the body, or such parts of it as had been eaten, must have been completely digested.   *(1)*

August, 1829

An extraordinary find was made in the Queen's Head Tavern, Rothersithe (U.K.). A servant girl purchased two oysters from a woman named Field and, on opening one of them, she saw something black adhering to the animal. She removed it, cleaned it and was amazed and delighted to find that it was a sovereign in perfect condition.

Excited people gathered around and closely examined the dead oyster and its shell. The figure of St. George and the Dragon were clearly impressed on the shell, whilst the belly of the fish showed a faint outline of the reverse side of the coin. The curious discovery was placed on exhibition in the tavern.

It was not known whether there was any quibbling regarding ownership of the coin but the legal position was thought to be fairly clear. The servant girl had purchased the oyster, so surely she was also entitled to the coin. *The Times* report mentioned that oysters, at the ebb tide, always lay with the shell partly open. Somehow, the coin must have dropped or bounced into the shell at that time. *(2)*

April, 1837.

It was a lucky day for a woman, described as a poor widow, residing at Hollywell Colliery (U.K.), when she bought a small fish from a travelling fish hawker for one penny. She found inside it half a sovereign. *(3)*

December, 1840

An Edinburgh man purchased a cod and because of the enormous size of its belly, hoped to find a large roe in it. In this he was disappointed but he continued to cut and was astonished to find in its stomach an entire fresh teal duck, with hardly a feather ruffled. Both the cod and the duck were devoured for dinner. *(4)*

Other Surprising Contents

There seems to be almost no end to the variety of things that can be found in the stomachs of fish. In 1844 a cod was caught at Invergarden (U.K.) and in his stomach was a silver-handled pen-knife in perfect condition, the carving on its handle an example of beautiful workmanship. *(5)*

In 1855 a rabbit's foot was found in a ling's stomach and an entire kitten inside a cod caught at Kirkwall Bay (U.K.). *(6)*

The Connecticut Mirror reported in June, 1820, that a bass weighing 55 to 60 pounds had been caught off Haddam and that, on opening it, a full bottle of rum was found which presumably must have been accidentally dropped from some vessel.

At Cape May in 1928 when a 4-pound "croaker" was hooked the fishermen heard a ticking noise coming from it as it was brought aboard. On opening it, they found a watch which one of the men had accidentally dropped over the side not long before. *(7)*

A 16-pound eel, caught in Rocky Creek, Dorrigo, N.S.W. (Australia), in November, 1934, was found to contain a partly-digested rabbit. *(8)*

At Boston in 1939 the trawler *Arlington* reported that the crew had found in the mouth of a 20-pound cod a notebook 6 inches by 3 inches in size which had evidently belonged to a man named Molo Luigi Razza. His name was at the front of the book, which contained notes relevant to the freezing of fish. *(9)*

Half a coconut was found inside a 16-pound cod caught off Lowestoft (U.K.) in February, 1967. *(10)*

A Sydney (Australia) man caught a 2-pound bream at Kirra, Queensland, and inside it was a 1947 two-shilling piece. The coin was tarnished but still in good condition. *(11)*

September, 1848

The skipper of a sloop from Rothesay (U.K.), which was anchored at Lochbroom in 1848, experienced such a strange coincidence that he could not have been blamed for wondering whether supernatural influences were at work.

Whilst at Lochbroom, he spent some time fishing over the side of the vessel and, while so engaged, he dropped a bunch of keys into 10 fathoms of water. Attached to the keys was a piece of parchment on which he had written his name and the name of the vessel. Naturally, he assumed the keys were lost for all time.

Six weeks later the vessel dropped anchor off the island of Rassay, which is about 100 miles from Lochbroom. Once again the skipper resumed his favourite spare-time pursuit of fishing. He caught, among other fish, a large codfish, which he unhooked and threw on the deck. To his amazement, as the fish gave vent to its last convulsive movements, it coughed onto the deck the skipper's lost bunch of keys. There could be no mistake. The parchment with the names of the skipper and the sloop, still partly preserved, proved the point.

As well as the keys, the cod also disgorged a penknife belonging to a fellow skipper. Identification of the skipper was made possible by the initials engraved on the knife.   *(12)*

May, 1865

Some fish seem to have stranger appetites than others. One that seemed to have been happy to swallow practically anything it could get its mouth around was a grouper that was caught off the coast of Queensland, Australia. It was a big specimen, 7 feet long and 6 feet in circumference at the thickest part of its body. The head weighed 80 pounds. Its stomach contained two broken bottles, a quart pot, a preserved milk tin, 7 medium-sized crabs, a 3-inch piece of earthenware triangular in shape and encrusted with oyster shells, a sheep's head, some mutton and beef bones and a few loose oyster shells. The spine of a skate was embedded in its liver.   *(13)*

August, 1872

In this instance, which was reported in San Francisco in August, 1872, there was a strong suspicion that the fish did not actually gobble up the strange things that were found inside them. There was something fishy going on.

In those days newspapers did not have to worry much about being accused of racism, or being sued for libel, so the *San Francisco Bulletin* was able to refer to what it termed a company of the "Heathen Chinee" and to voice its suspicions quite bluntly about what they had been up to.

The Bulletin explained that the Chinese had been engaged in catching mountain trout at Lake Tahoe and selling them at the San Francisco market. It went on:

> Recently the profits of second dealers have been rendered precarious, in consequence of the tendency of mountain trout to feed on such non-nutritious substances as scrap iron. The railroad spikes, rail clamps etc. found in the stomachs of these fish are of modern pattern, precisely similar to those used on the Central Pacific Railroad and as the trout do not come ashore in pursuit of such diet, it is presumed that the Chinese engaged in their capture know some explanation of the mystery. The fish sell at 35 cents per pound and it is not uncommon to find in some of the specimens pieces of iron weighing as much as the fish itself. *(14)*

December, 1930

A 10-foot shark that was caught off Watson's Bay, N.S.W. (Australia), was found to have in its stomach a woman's handbag. In it were the ordinary kind of items one would expect such as a comb, pencil and powder puff. But there was also one other surprising item – a wristlet watch that was still ticking. *(15)*

April, 1932

On September 25, 1925 the Lord Mayor of Liverpool (U.K.) cast a ring into the sea just outside the estuary of the Mersey to celebrate the symbolic marriage of that city to the sea. Two days later the trawler *Salvor* fished the ring up from the depths and brought it back, much to the consternation of the Lord Mayor and the Corporation. We are not told whether they threw it back into the water again. *(16a)*

A Scot caught a trout in Loch Lannish in 1932 and found inside it a gold wedding ring. *(16b)*

The best story about a ring inside a fish, however, concerns an incident that occurred during the 1920's on a train in Germany. Two Englishmen happened to be sitting opposite each other during a journey. Let's call them Smith and Jones. Jones was wearing an unusual ring and Smith's eyes were continually drawn to it. Finally, Smith could contain his curiosity no longer. He said, "Could you tell me about that ring. I once owned one just like it."

"I bought it from a fishmonger in Yarmouth," explained Jones. "He found it whilst cleaning a cod."

"Is there an inscription inside the ring saying, 'From an unhappy Queen'?" asked Smith.

Jones, much astonished, confirmed that this was so.

Smith explained that he had lost the ring whilst deep-sea fishing off the Norfolk coast. It had been given to one of his ancestors by Queen Caroline.

Jones, of course, returned the ring to its rightful owner. *(16c)*

February, 1938

In 1935 John Gallon, Jnr, lost a chain to which was attached a silver pocket-knife, his wife's wedding ring, a religious medal and his name plate. Three years later John Gallon caught a 3-pound pickerel which contained the keepsakes in its stomach, complete, and none the worse for wear. *(17)*

April, 1938

When Walter Casson, Jnr, aged 13, of Torrington, Connecticut, went fishing for the first time in his life, he had a wonderfully successful day. He caught nine large trout. One of the fish measured 11 inches in length and whilst dressing it the boy found two valuable Lincoln-head pennies. *(18)*

August, 1938

A most mysterious item was found inside a fish by Mr L.R. Russell, of Miami, Florida, in August, 1938. Mr Russell landed a 12-pound grouper and as he removed the hook from its mouth the object came out with the hook. It was a shell on which the Lord's Prayer had been engraved. *(19)*

April, 1939

A Maori, fishing in the Tarawera River, New Zealand, made a grisly discovery inside the stomach of an eel he had caught – two human fingers!

The Maori handed the fingers to the police, who soon solved the mystery. A man working on the Tarawera Bridge, three miles from the spot where the eel was caught, had severely injured his hand. When blood poisoning set in he amputated the fingers himself with an axe before setting out to get treatment from the nearest doctor. And, of course, he threw the severed fingers into the river. *(20)*

September, 1945

Louis McIntyre, a policeman from Beloit, Wisconsin, went on a fishing vacation to Rhinelander, in the northern part of the state. He returned home happy, with a big fish, a trophy, and a story to tell.

The fish was a 22 pound muskellunge. The trophy was a full bottle of beer which had been found in the fish's stomach. McIntyre said that the fish had battled for 35 minutes before he managed to get it ashore. *(21)*

June, 1949

A 14-foot crocodile was caught near the meatworks at Wyndham, Western Australia, and inside it was found a gold signet ring which bore the initials "J.T.".

The find almost certainly resolved a mystery concerning a missing man: a young Englishman, a refrigeration engineer, was believed to have drowned when he accidentally walked off a stepway on the meat-cargo ship *Kent* on July 6, 1948. His body was never found. The man's name was John Thompson. *(22)*

June, 1949

A diner at an oyster bar in Melbourne (Australia) had a lucky find when he ordered a dozen oysters. As he sank his teeth into the 11th oyster he found that he was biting on something hard. It was a pearl, quite a valuable one, which a jeweller later valued at £65.

The lucky man was Fred Yarr, a milk bar proprietor. He told friends that he would not be interested in selling the pearl. "I wouldn't take £650 for it," he said. "I'm not going to throw away my luck. I'm going to have the pearl polished up and it will make a beautiful tie-pin." *(23)*

December, 1952

During 1952 a couple of unusual crocodiles were killed in Uganda. One had a 15-foot python in its stomach. The other croc was unusual because of its enormous size. It was 19 feet 6 inches long and 4 feet 9 inches wide across the belly. Both of the crocodiles were caught in the Semliki River. *(24)*

December, 1956

Whilst enjoying his Christmas Day dinner in 1956, Mr Jean Judin of Rennes, Brittany (France), opened an oyster and found inside it a gold coin. It was a 10-franc golden Louis bearing the inscription "Napoleon III, 1859".

The coin appeared to have been in the oyster for a long time, for the shell had a circular brown mark of the same size. *(25)*

1982

An unusual lost and found incident occurred on the Coomera River, south of Brisbane (Australia), a few years ago.

A young lady was water-skiing on the river when she lost her sparkling new diamond engagement ring. The story spread quickly among the local populace but, of course, the chances of recovering it seemed almost zero. Then, a local fisherman caught a big flathead, opened it, and there was the ring. (26)

November, 1988

A sailor named Gosselin Deleus, from England, was just as lucky as the lady mentioned above when he accidentally dropped his £150 spectacles into the sea in 1988.

He read in the paper some time later that a Belgian fisherman had found a pair of glasses in the belly of a 13-pound monkfish. Deleus wrote to the fisherman, and, sure enough, the serial number on the glasses proved that they were his. (27)

January, 1989

An equally incredible coincidence was experienced by Alain Vigneron, a Frenchman who was employed as a butler in England. Vigneron frequently went to sea on fishing expeditions with three of his friends. On one such outing during 1988 the sea blew up rough and Vigneron became sea-sick. In his misery, he spewed his dentures into the ocean.

Six months later he and his friends went to the same fishing spot again and he told them jokingly that he would probably fish up his teeth. Not long after arriving there, he reeled in a 4-pound cod, cut it open, and there were his dentures!

"I nearly fell over with surprise," said Alain. "I showed them to my friends and we all stood around with our mouths open. I never thought I'd see those teeth again. And then to find them like that! It's incredible."

The teeth were somewhat the worse for wear and Alain will never be able to wear them again. But, as he said, "They're the best fishing trophy any man could ever have." (28)

October, 1989

Randy Lindquist, of Randolph, Vermont, lost his wallet overboard during a deep-sea fishing trip on the Atlantic Ocean. Six days later, it was found by two other fishermen, who mailed it back to him. Everything was still in the wallet, unharmed, including credit cards, driver's licence and $93 in cash.

Said Lindquist, "I don't know what the odds were against the wallet ever being hooked in the open ocean of the Atlantic. They have to be mind-boggling. I had better odds trying to hit the Megabucks lottery than ever seeing it again."

Dennis Murphy described how he and his son found the wallet: "Jim and I were trolling for bluefish on the seaward side of the Isle of Shoals off the New Hampshire coast. The ocean depth was about 140 feet.

"Jim was checking the lines periodically for seaweed, and during one of those checks he found that instead of a bluefish, we'd hooked somebody's wallet."

The wallet had moved with the tide and was found about three miles further out to sea from the spot where Lindquist had dropped it.   *(29)*

The Shark Arm Case

One of the most famous cases in the annals of Australian crime is a murder that is generally referred to as "The Shark Arm Case".

The story began on April 25, 1935 when a shark disgorged a man's arm into the water in the Coogee Aquarium, Sydney. The 14-foot tiger shark had been caught eight days earlier and immediately placed on exhibition.

In those days there was not the same forensic expertise that is available today but the police were aided in their efforts to identify the victim by the fact that there were tattoo-marks on the arm. Using these, and later finger-prints, the body was identified

84

as that of James Smith, a 45-year-old man who had been missing from his home since April 8. Police established that Smith had been murdered shortly after he went missing and that his dismembered body had been dumped at sea in a trunk.

We will not go into the details of the case here but it became clear that the murder had resulted from an underworld feud and that drug trafficking had been involved.

One interesting point was that a suspect named Brady successfully appealed to the Supreme Court to prevent the coroner from continuing with the inquest on Smith on the ground that he had no jurisdiction to hold an inquiry on an arm. Under a statute of 1276, a single limb could not be considered a body and the finding of a body was essential to an inquest.

The story returned to the headlines again and again as further developments unfolded, including another murder, police chases and sensational trials, but the case was never really unravelled.

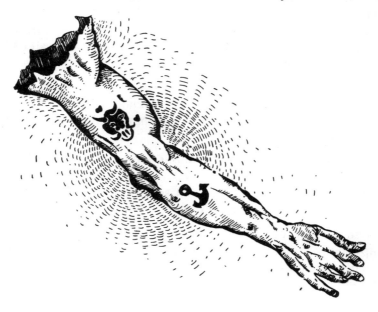

7. Dolphin Stories

Dolphins are not fish, of course; they are mammals. However, as mentioned earlier, I have interpreted the term "fish" very loosely when selecting stories for this book. My interpretation of the term has been "aquatic animals".

There is no doubt that there is a special affinity between dolphins and man. This has been well recognised (and recorded) for at least 2,000 years. Dolphins have shown in battles with sharks and killer whales that they can be fierce fighters; and yet there is not one recorded case of a dolphin being hostile towards man – even though many dolphins have been hunted and killed by men.

Not only that, but there have been scores, probably hundreds, of recorded instances where humans in adversity have been aided by dolphins. People who were drowning, for instance, have been pushed to the shore. Some scientists have warned that we may be making too much of such instances, that they may not have been due to any conscious desire on the part of the dolphins to help humans. Dolphins have been seen to push water-logged mattresses ashore as well.

Be that as it may, some of the stories that follow are of occasions when dolphins do appear to have deliberately helped people. Readers can make up their own minds about the dolphin's motivation in these instances.

If there was ever any question about it, one thing that has become clear from the study of dolphins during the past two or three decades is that they have a great sense of fun. And they love a human audience. In fact, they are real hams.

When Dr Lilly, of Florida, jumped into a dolphin tank one day he happened to dog-paddle. Immediately, a dolphin swung round, faced him, and began to mimic him by flapping its flippers in a "pat-a-cake" fashion. *(1)*

The point about the story was that the dolphin's action was completely spontaneous. It was not doing something that it had been taught.

Another dolphin took over an aquaplane so that he could experience the pleasure of being towed behind a boat. Dr Horace Dobbs, who had been studying a wild dolphin named Donald for some time, said that the dolphin put in an appearance soon after the tow began.

"When I refused to let go," said Dr Dobbs, "he bit my arm progressively harder until I had to release the handle. Then he grabbed the board in his mouth and enjoyed a tow behind the boat." *(2)*

A dolphin in Florida's Marineland amused himself by rolling a large turtle over and over along the floor of the tank, from one side wall to the other. Then he repeated the performance. *(3)*

The dolphins at Marineland are always making up new games. One dolphin, named Frankie, played a game of "fetching" with a member of the public. First, he picked up a pebble about 1 inch in size from the bottom of the tank and threw it to a man standing close by. The man threw the pebble back into the pool, whereupon Frankie retrieved it and threw it back to him. This procedure was repeated eight times, each time with the same man, although there were plenty of other people leaning against the railing. *(4)*

There was one occasion when a dolphin named Donald, whom we have already mentioned, made it perfectly clear that he wished to help his human friend. Dr Dobbs had lost a brand-new, under-water camera and was searching for it when Donald began to nudge him, then swam off. Dr Dobbs followed the dolphin. Donald then suspended himself in the water, head down, like a giant arrow, pointing at the lost camera. *(5)*

* * * * *

The November, 1949 issue of *Natural History Magazine* told the story of how a dolphin saved the life of a drowning woman by pushing her ashore. The woman had gone swimming alone on a private beach and, while wading in waist-deep water, she was caught by an undertow and swept off her feet. She swallowed water and was not able to make any headway against the current.

Later, when describing her experience, she said, "I realised that, while only about ten feet from shore, there was no way I could make it, and kept thinking, as I gradually lost consciousness, please God, can't someone push me ashore. With that, someone gave me a tremendous shove, and I landed on the beach, face down, too exhausted to turn over."

It was several minutes before she recovered sufficiently to turn around and when she did so she saw a dolphin close to the shore, leaping about. A few feet beyond the dolphin was a "large fish".

At this stage a man ran onto the scene from the nearby public beach. He corroborated the last part of the woman's story. He had seen what he thought was a dead body being pushed ashore by a dolphin. He thought that the dolphin was protecting the body from a shark.   (6)

* * * * *

In December, 1968 solo yachtsman, Bernard Moitessier, was sailing near Stewart Island in the *Joshua* when the sky became overcast. He continued on what he was sure was a safe course, one which should have taken him well clear of the outlying reefs about the island. Then, suddenly, he was surrounded by dolphins. There must have been at least 100 of them. But what amazed him most was their behaviour.

A line of 25 dolphins, swimming side by side, passed the *Joshua*, then, still in formation, they swung hard right.

"I watch, wonderstruck. More than ten times they repeat the same thing ... I have never seen such a perfect ballet. And each time, it is to the right that they rush off, whipping the sea white for 30 yards. They are obeying a precise command, that is for

88

sure. I can't tell if it is always the same group of 20 or 25; there are too many dolphins to keep track. They seem nervous; I do not understand."

Then Moitessier looked at his compass and he did understand. "*Joshua* is running downwind at seven knots straight for Stewart Island, hidden in the stratus. The steady west wind had shifted around to the south without my realising it. The course change was not apparent." Moitessier corrected the yacht's course in time to avoid the threatened disaster.

"And then something wonderful happens: a big black and white dolphin jumps ten or twelve feet in the air in a fantastic somersault, with two complete rolls. And he lands flat, tail forward. Three times he does this double roll, bursting with a tremendous joy, as if he were shouting to me and all the other dolphins: 'The man understood that we were trying to tell him to sail to the right ... you understood ... you understood.' "   *(7)*

* * * * *

A 12-foot dolphin became well known to local divers in Mount's Bay, Cornwall, England, during the 1970's. He was a bit of a rascal, full of curiosity and mischief and the divers named him Beaky.

One day he became a hero when he saved the life of one of the divers. Keith Monery, a 24-year old diving student, found that his life-jacket was leaking. He had heavy equipment strapped to his back and was not able to keep himself above water. He began to panic, thrashed about and gave the other divers the standard distress signal as he sank beneath the water.

Two diving instructors, Bob and Hazel Carswell, responded immediately to the signal. Hazel dived in and swam towards the student while Bob jumped into a boat. As Hazel swam towards Monery she saw a large shape flash past underneath her. It was Beaky. He reached Monery long before Hazel, nudged the diver upwards to the surface, and supported him there for several minutes until Hazel arrived.

Beaky continued to help them, nudging them upwards and pushing them towards safety until Bob arrived in the boat.   (8)

* * * * *

Kobus Stander, a South African, told the story in 1978 of how he and three other fishermen, were saved by dolphins when they were engulfed by heavy fog off Dassen Island.

"I have never experienced such heavy fog," said Kobus. "We could not see more than two metres away from the boat. We had no idea where we were."

Suddenly a number of dolphins appeared around the craft. "They began nudging the boat towards the left, and Mr Macgregor was convinced that the dolphins were trying to steer us in a certain direction," said Kobus. "I had just swung the boat to the left when we heard waves breaking, and through the gap in the fog I could see the rocks. We would have hit them if we had not turned. Another three minutes and we would have had it. This convinced us, so we let the dolphins lead us. Two of them stayed on each side of the boat, bumping on the side when they wanted us to go in a certain direction. We were sailing blind, but by then we had full faith in our helpers."

When the boat reached calm water the dolphins changed their swimming pattern. "They all began swimming around the boat, as though they wanted us to go no further. They would not let us go in any direction, blocking our way. I decided to drop anchor, and this seemed to satisfy them. They swam around us for a while, jumped and frolicked as though they were happy, then disappeared."

Gradually the fog cleared and the fishermen found, to their surprise, that they were in the sheltered bay at Ysterfontein, the place from which they had originally set out. *(9)*

* * * * *

There was one occasion during World War II when efforts by a number of dolphins to help humans were not appreciated at all. The story was told by Dr George Llano in his book *Airmen Against the Sea*. Six downed American flyers were drifting on a rubber raft, not far from a Japanese-occupied island, when several dolphins turned up. To the dismay of the Americans, the dolphins insisted on pushing the raft towards the island. Eventually, the dolphins had to be forcibly driven off. *(10)*

* * * * *

An incident was observed in October, 1954 where a dolphin in trouble was helped by others of his kin. A stick of dynamite had been exploded under water and a dolphin was stunned. Immediately, two other adult dolphins raced to its aid. They placed their heads under its flippers and held its nose above the surface. Periodically, they would break off from this task to get a breath of air themselves. At these times, it appeared to the observers that the task of supporting the stunned dolphin was taken over by another pair of dolphins. Or perhaps it was the same pair back again. The seas were rough and the observers could not be sure. *(11)*

* * * * *

An amazing dolphin-rescue story was told in the *National Enquirer* of April 19, 1988 by Peter Stock, one of the participants in the drama.

Stock, with two companions, Roger Hilligan and Terry MacDonald, was sailing his 16-foot catamaran in the Indian Ocean, about a mile off the east coast of South Africa, when the craft was capsized by a sudden, fierce storm. All three occupants were thrown into the water.

Immediately, ten dolphins appeared and began circling around the three men, as if to protect them. The dolphins made high-pitched, squealing noises as though they were communicating with each other.

Peter Stock was holding on to a rope dangling from the catamaran when a big wave swept the craft about 300 yards away. He maintained his grip on the rope and therefore became separated from his companions. As Stock was swept away, four dolphins darted off from the main pack and joined him.

"I managed to crawl up the rope and get aboard the boat," said Stock. "I was exhausted. But the boat capsized again and I was thrown back into the water. I was so dazed and tired I felt like giving up and letting death take me. But one dolphin immediately put its nose under my backside and started pushing me toward the boat! It was an amazing feeling – as if some giant hand were picking me up and lifting me along. The dolphin pushed me right to the boat, and I began dragging myself aboard."

But Stock's troubles were far from over. Two sharks suddenly put in an appearance nearby. "Then, to my amazement," he said, "I saw three of the dolphins go after the two sharks, while the fourth dolphin stayed behind with me, so close I could touch it. It seemed as if he were saying, 'Don't worry – you'll be safe with me.'" Two dolphins rammed one shark in the side whilst the third dolphin raced at the other shark, obviously intent on doing the same. The sharks decided they had had enough. They swung around and fled.

Stock set off to swim to the shore, pushing the boat in front of him. And, all the way, the four dolphins accompanied him. Periodically, a dolphin would speed off, sweep around in a big circle on patrol, evidently searching for sharks, then return making strange sounds of communication to his friends.

When Stock arrived on the shore he found that his two companions were also safe. They had swum to the beach with the other 6 dolphins spread out protectively around them all the way.

The story told by the three men was corroborated by a number of people, including Nigel Fairhead, a Cape Town shoe store owner, who watched the whole thing from shore with binoculars.   *(12)*

* * * * *

Not only is there a strange rapport between dolphins and man: a similar rapport apparently exists between dolphins and man's best friend, dogs. Wade Doak has documented in his *Dolphin Dolphin* a number of instances where this bond was evident.

In all these instances the dogs showed no unusual interest in fish, no matter how large or small, sharks, or even a whale. But, with dolphins it was different. They seemed to know instinctively that the dolphins were their friends.

The best story was told by Ted Boehler, a top American scuba diver, about an incident near Santa Catalina Island involving his small dog, Oro.

About 30 to 40 dolphins appeared near the boat and the dog got very excited. He whined just as he does when he is on the leash and sees another dog that he wishes to play with. Next thing, he jumped overboard and began cavorting with the dolphins.

Ted Boehler quickly donned his diving gear, grabbed his underwater camera, and dived into the water to join them. For 20 minutes the dog and the dolphins played together. The dog was fascinated by the dolphins and the dolphins were equally fascinated by the dog. The dolphins would circle Oro, leap about in the water around him and do barrel-rolls underneath him.

And all of this was captured on film by Ted Boehler.   *(13)*

* * * * *

This time, just for a change, it was the dolphins who needed help – from humans. On October 8, 1967 a group of dolphins surrounded a fishing boat and began pushing it towards a buoy that was floating nearby. The fishermen quickly got the message and moved across to the buoy to investigate. They found that a young dolphin had got itself trapped in the anchorline and that manipulation of the rope by human hands was necessary to free it. The fishermen released the dolphin and, immediately, all members of the dolphin troop showed their gratitude by giving vent to a chorus of joyous, high-pitched whistles and by leaping about the boat. *(14)*

* * * * *

Another incident was recorded, in 1988, where a dolphin asked for human aid. But, unfortunately, on this occasion there was nothing the humans could do.

Vincent Galazzo, skipper of a fishing boat, said he was operating in the Mediterranean, off the French Riviera, when a dolphin came alongside his boat and nudged its bow, as though trying to change the boat's direction. Then the dolphin would swim off in the direction he wished the boat to take. Curious, Galazzo turned the nose of his craft after the dolphin.

"We followed the dolphin for several hundred yards," he said. "He knew exactly where he was taking us. Ahead of us was a badly injured female dolphin barely floating in the water. Her dorsal fin had been almost torn off and there was blood in the water. The male raced on to her and used his body to keep her from sinking. He kept pushing her toward us, crying out to us all the time. She probably had been hit by a power boat. The wound was very deep ... and we realised she was already dead. It was very sad. The male dolphin didn't seem to accept that his mate was dead. He was obviously hoping that we could save her." *(15)*

8. You Wouldn't Believe It!

October, 1787

A fish once saved a sailing ship from disaster. The story was told in *The Times* of October 13, 1787. We are not told the name of the ship but it was described as a packet-boat which was returning from Holland to England in the year 1709. The ship struck very bad weather and was so violently buffeted about by storms that she sprang a leak. The pumps were manned but the water continued to pour in faster than it could be pumped out. The hold filled and the passengers and crew had almost given themselves up as lost when, to the wonderment of the people, the water stopped coming in.

On arrival back at their home port, the ship was examined and it was found that the hole had been plugged by a large fish being sucked into it. *(1)*

August, 1808

The death was recorded in August, 1808 of an old trout which had been the sole tenant of a well in Dumbarton Castle for more than 28 years. It had been caught in the River Leven and placed in the well by an officer of the military garrison that was stationed there. It was adopted as a kind of military mascot and soon became so tame that it would accept bread and other food from the hands of the soldiers. It weighed a pound when first caught and, strangely enough, despite being well fed throughout its life, it never grew any bigger. A suggestion at the time was that this was probably due to the quality of the water in which it lived. Perhaps this was the explanation, or perhaps the small size of its living area was a factor. During its declining years the trout became literally grey around the mouth and nostrils. *(2)*

December, 1824

It is a strange fact that eels, for some unknown reason, display a marked behavioural change during periods of high winds. Why should this be so? They live beneath the surface of the water where one would think that they would be insulated from atmospheric conditions. Nevertheless, they are so affected and this has been known to be a fact for centuries.

It was reported in 1824 that the Scottish community at Linlithgow were in an excellent position to take advantage of this phenomenon and that they had been doing so for generations. The town adjoined a loch and the stream that flowed from the loch at the west end passed through a sluice, then fell into an artificial reservoir, from which it escaped through a number of holes in the sides and bottom. Whether by accident or design, these holes were too small to allow average-sized eels to pass through, so the reservoir served the purpose of an eel trap.

In calm weather, however, eels were rarely caught in the trap. But, when strong winds blew, especially from the west, the eels seemed to be seized by a mad panic and they would rush from the loch like animals fleeing from a bushfire.

During one period of high winds in 1824 the local populace removed a cart-load of eels from the reservoir every day and, on one particular day, two cart-loads. *(3)*

August, 1839

A line baited with a worm was put into the Hay mill-stream, in the United Kingdom. Next morning the fisherman discovered that he had caught an eel as well as a jack. The eel had been caught first but, while still hooked, it had been swallowed by the jack. Still alive, inside the jack, the eel attempted to chew his way to freedom. He managed to get partially through one of the jack's gills, but at that point he got stuck and that was the end for both of them.

The jack was ultimately landed without a hook in him at all. He was 2 feet 4 inches long and weighed 8 pounds. The eel was a little over a foot in length. *(4)*

August, 1843

A gamekeeper was walking alongside the waters of Laggan, Scotland, accompanied by his dog, a fine, big Newfoundland cross-breed, when the animal suddenly got very excited. The sight that had attracted the dog's attention was a beautiful salmon which was cavorting in the water in a well-known fishing hole at Corrary Bridge, near Bowmore. Next moment, the dog plunged into the water and swam after his quarry. After a short, successful struggle, the dog brought ashore a fine fish which weighed 14 pounds.

His owner said that the canine fisherman had performed similar feats on a number of previous occasions. *(5)*

January, 1847

An unusual scene was witnessed by several government officials during December, 1846 on the Findhorn River in Scotland. There was an unusual commotion among the spawning beds and, on coming closer, they discovered that it was a fight to the death between two male salmon for possession of a female. The female was close by, watching the combat, and the officials said they had never seen two adversaries of any species fight a fiercer battle. The water was lashed to a foam and stained red with blood.

Then, the water calmed and one of the salmon floated to the surface, dead. The men recovered its body and found that the flesh had been ripped off its back from head to tail.

Local fishermen said that males had often been seen chasing one another in the spawning grounds but none had ever witnessed a fight such as this. *(6)*

November, 1847

It was reported in *The Times* that Mr Lister Smith, of Bocking (U.K.), had in his fish pond several perch which he had been able to tame to a surprising degree. He had caught them during the previous spring and had taught them to come when they were called and to eat from the hands of his children.

He told of one of these perch which made a glutton of itself by gorging 31 worms in one gulp. It disappeared for 10 or 12 days after that and Mr Smith feared that it had gorged itself to death. However, it returned again, but seemed to have learnt its lesson in that it ate more sparingly, limiting itself to five or six worms at a time. *(7)*

November, 1854

At Salcombe (U.K.) a ferryman watched as a cormorant dived into the water, then began struggling as though in great difficulties. The ferryman rowed over to investigate and found that half of the bird had been swallowed by a large monkfish. The ferryman grabbed hold of both of them and, hoping to save the life of the bird, he cut open the fish. It was to no avail, however, for the bird died soon after. The fish weighed 10 pounds. *(8)*

October, 1856

The 500-ton sailing ship, *Cuban*, survived what the crew believed was a deliberate attack on it by a gigantic whale.

The ship was travelling at 10 knots when there was a tremendous shock which caused the vessel to heel over and then come to a sudden stop. Men who were sleeping were thrown right out of their bunks.

Shortly after, the whale surfaced near the ship. It appeared stunned for a few moments, then recovered and swam towards the *Cuban*, as if intending to attack it again. Then, the whale apparently changed its mind for it wheeled around and dived. As it did so, its tail rose 30 to 40 feet and threw a large quantity of blood and water onto the deck.

The whale was heard blowing just before the crash. Because of this, and also because of the tremendous force of the collision, the captain and crew were sure that the whale was not asleep and that it did attack deliberately. *(9)*

September, 1858

An unusual struggle was witnessed between a duck and an eel in a small stream at Arran, Scotland. Someone had thrown the entrails of a fish into the stream and the two animals disputed ownership of the tasty morsel. The duck got to it first and proceeded to swallow it. Then it found that a large eel had taken hold of the other end of the delicacy. The eel won the contest in the end, but not before the duck had twice been pulled completely under the water. *(10)*

September, 1862

A large thorough-bred bulldog found he had taken on more than he bargained for in Montreal one evening in September, 1862 when he attacked a big lobster. The dog was passing a store when his attention was attracted by some movement in front of the door. He investigated, found it was a lobster and immediately advanced upon it. But lobsters are not defenceless creatures and this one extended its large powerful claws and showed plenty of fight.

First it got hold of the dog's leg; then it switched its grip to his tail. At this point the dog lost interest in the fight and attempted to run away, but the lobster held on grimly. The dog ran yelping down the street, dragging the lobster behind him.

Some people, who were nearby, then intervened and detached the determined, 27-pound crustacean, following which the dog bolted off at top speed. *(11)*

November, 1864

It was reported from Cuba that an eight-year-old boy had been carried off by a cuttlefish. A number of children came across the fish on the beach and attacked it with sticks and stones. The fish hurriedly retreated to the sea but as it reached the water's edge, it flung out a tentacle at the nearest boy, grabbed hold of him, and began dragging him into the ocean. The boy screamed and struggled but to no avail. Some bigger boys ran to help him but they were too late. His body had disappeared from sight. *(12)*

August, 1874

A correspondent to *The New York Times* in August, 1874 told of how one particular species of fish had roused his sympathies to such an extent that he threw one back into the sea. His letter read:

> That the imperfect voice of the fish is used to express discontent and pain I have no doubt, as in numerous

experiments on a fish found in the Gulf of Mexico, called the grunt, I found that the voice was used and modulated as with other animals. When touched with the knife the grunts that it gave vent to fairly rose to a shriek, and when dying its moans and sobs were almost disagreeably human. I shall never forget the first one of these veritable porkers that I caught. Thinking that my bait needed replenishing, I hauled in and found, nicely hooked, a grunt. No sooner had I placed him in the boat than he commenced a series of grunts and sobs that bade fair to take me by storm. Now he would make a low noise, and gradually swell the "melody", and finally hurl at me such a blast of entreaties, all of which were produced without a struggle, that my better nature was aroused, and I made haste to toss him back, and as he disappeared he uttered a squeak which, together with the splash, sounded to me like a "thank you", and I have no doubt but what it was. *(13)*

December, 1874

The Aquarium of the Zoological Station at Naples experienced problems during 1874 caused by large numbers of rats invading the premises. Not only did they do considerable damage to the woodwork but they attacked and killed many animals.

One animal which showed that it was well able to defend itself against the marauders was an octopus which caught and killed a number of rats. All that would be left of them in the morning were the bones and sometimes a part of the skin. *(14)*

May, 1875

Miss Adelaide Miller, a Hawaiian singing star of the 1870's, was swimming one day with some of her girlfriends at a local beach when someone dared her to swim out to a reef quite some distance off. She accepted the challenge, set off, and the other girls followed her.

They were swimming in deep water when some men in a nearby canoe began shouting, "Mano! Mano!", which, as they well knew, meant shark. Soon after, a great shape came to the surface right under Miss Miller and she found herself sitting on the shark's back. She decided the best thing to do was to stay where she was so she grasped the shark's upper fin and held on tight.

The shark, probably just as surprised as his passenger, skimmed across the surface of the water at top speed for about 60 yards. Then, he dived suddenly, leaving Miss Miller behind at the surface. She and the other girls were picked up by canoes before the shark returned.   *(15)*

May, 1875

When Captain John O. Holmes returned from a cruise among the Society Islands in 1875, he told of how a woman had saved her life by spending a night out in the open sea on the back of a turtle.

The story began when Captain Holmes sailed his vessel into a small cove in search of water and fresh food. As usual, the ship was visited by a crowd of local natives, some of whom wished to trade, others merely to socialise. Among them was an attractive 18-year-old girl, the daughter of the local chief, and it quickly became evident that she and the ship's mate were strongly attracted to each other.

Two days later the couple were married, a great feast being held to celebrate the event. The captain performed the ceremony to solemnise the occasion, but only grudgingly because he knew the girl would have to accompany her new husband on the voyage home and he was upset about the unseemliness of a having a woman on board his ship.

The bride's name was Wi-Wi, meaning "Big Fish" or "Great Swimmer", and she quickly settled down to life on board the vessel.

One evening, as Wi-Wi was at the bow of the ship bathing herself with water scooped from the sea, the ship unexpectedly dipped forward into the water and she was washed overboard. The dread cry rang out from the look-out: "Man overboard!" although, of course, in this case it was a woman.

The mate, with several men, launched a boat and began searching for Wi-Wi, but it was becoming darker with every minute and, eventually, they had to admit defeat and return to the ship. The ship hove to, and the crew called out, continually, all night but received no response.

Everyone except the mate had given the girl up for lost by morning, but the mate, understandably, was determined to carry on the search. He sighted a dark object in the sea some distance off. "It's only a turtle," said one of the crew. Nevertheless, a boat was launched to investigate. As they drew close they could see it was a turtle, a giant turtle – and sitting on its back was Wi-Wi!

She said, later, that after swimming about for some time she came across the turtle, which was floating complacently on the surface, and climbed onto its back. The turtle did not seem to mind its passenger at all.

Back in San Francisco, as Captain Holmes finished telling his story, one of his listeners asked, "And what of the turtle that came along so providentially and enabled the young woman to survive?" The captain admitted, guiltily, that it had been towed back to the ship and that the animal had ended up as turtle soup. *(16)*

April, 1880

That fish do have reasoning powers and memory, was confidently asserted by Mr Seth Green, the Superintendent of the New York State Fish Hatchery. Mr Green said he was convinced of this because of experiments he had carried out over a period of five years.

The fish that were the subject of the experiments were 5,000 large brook trout, all of which had been captured with the fly in unfrequented lakes and water courses in the Adirondack region five years previously, and which were then placed in No. 1 pond at the hatchery.

When the fish were hooked and slowly reeled to the boats they must have paid particular attention to the shape of the rod and tackle that were used in their capture and they never forgot their frightening experience with that apparatus.

Mr Green became a familiar sight to the fish as he walked about the pond and, for the purpose of the experiments, he would hide behind his back a walking stick and a fishing rod. When he revealed the walking stick to the fish by holding it out over the water, they would pay no attention to it. But, the moment he produced the rod and its tackle, the fish would rush off to distant parts of the pond.

Mr Green said he would let anyone cast a fly in that pond for he was quite sure that none of the fish would go near it. *(17)*

September, 1896

An enraged swordfish is capable of inflicting severe damage on a wooden ship. One vessel that was the victim of such an attack was the brigantine *Irmgard* which arrived at San Francisco from Honolulu with a sword, which had broken off the creature on impact, protruding through its hull. The sword passed through the 5-inch planking on the port bow, and also through the 8-inch skin planking behind it. The planks were split for about one foot on each side and the tip of the sword protruded one inch into the hold. *(18)*

June, 1911

Professor Raoul Pictet, of Geneva, announced that he had successfully concluded a series of experiments which demonstrated that it is possible to suspend life for an indefinite period.

In one experiment he took some live goldfish, froze them in water to 20 degrees centigrade below zero, and left them in that condition for three months. Then he gradually warmed the blocks of ice and brought the fish back to life.

Professor Pictet said that he had also carried out freezing experiments on other animals, including frogs, snails and dogs, but his most spectacular successes to date had been with fresh-water fish. *(19)*

December, 1921

Captain G. Evered Poole, a Commissioner in what was then the Gold Coast, a British colony, reported a most unusual occurrence that had been witnessed by him whilst returning to his post during 1921 after having enjoyed a period of leave in Britain.

It happened while the ship was between Sierra Leone and Sekondi and was seen by all those on board. For more than an hour the vessel steamed through the scene of a terrible whale massacre. The water was red with blood and hundreds of the giant creatures could be seen on the surface of the water, obviously dead or dying. Those capable of moving could do so only very slowly.

Captain Poole speculated that the whales may have fallen victim to an attack by hordes of swordfish. Neither he, nor anyone else on board, had ever seen such a spectacle before. *(20)*

But, was it really a massacre? A few days after Captain Poole's story was published, a certain Mr Henry Balfour, who was able to demonstrate a most expert knowledge of marine life, argued convincingly that the witnesses had been completely mistaken in their assumptions.

First, said Mr Balfour, in these times of relentless hunting of whales, it would be most unusual to see a gathering of hundreds of the creatures. What would have brought them together? Obviously an exceptional supply of their favourite food. That would be the most likely explanation.

And this could explain the blood red colour of the sea. It is a fact well known to whalers that when there is a great abundance of the whale's favourite food the sea is often of a bright red colour for miles. One of the small Copepods *(Calanus)* is of a bright red colour, and *Clione limacina*, a small Pteropod, is bright purple and, when myriads of such organisms are massed together, they bring a strong red tint to the colour of the sea.

Were the whales really dead or dying? "I think not," said Mr Balfour. "They were moving sluggishly because they had gorged themselves so full of food that they could hardly move. My suggestion converts a thrilling, blood-curdling tragedy into a common-place domestic scene; but I venture to think that this interpretation is more accurate and more satisfying, especially for the whales." *(21)*

May, 1922

Harry Summerfield, a farmer in the Northern Territory, Australia, showed that he was an extremely resourceful man when he survived a fight with a large crocodile.

Summerfield's property was situated on the Alligator River (a misnomer from the early pioneering days for there are no alligators in Australia) and he was standing with his back to the river when the monster crocodile came quietly out of the water, seized him by the leg and dragged him into the river. Summerfield was unarmed and had nothing to fight with but his bare hands. This, he proceeded to do most effectively. He jammed his thumb into the crocodile's eye, forcing it to release him. But, before he could escape, the crocodile seized his right arm, breaking his wrist in the process. Summerfield then drove his left thumb into the crocodile's other eye. Blinded in both eyes, the reptile released him and he was able to escape to the bank.

Doctors later reported at Darwin that Summerfield had been badly mauled on the arms and one leg but that he was on the road to recovery. *(22)*

February, 1926

After a freak electrical storm at East Marion, Long Island, local people had a good talking point. It appeared that large numbers of good-sized fish had literally fallen from the sky.

Horace Manwaring, who lived on the North Road, quite a distance from the water, awoke the morning after the storm to see fish scattered over the snow in front of his house. The word spread quickly throughout the community. How to explain it? Had it rained fish? Had seagulls been frightened by something, sudden thunder perhaps, and dropped their meal? Had a waterspout picked up the fish and carried them away from the water before dropping them?

The various hypotheses were still being vigorously debated when a number of Polish farmers disclosed the true reason. They had customarily used ling, a coarse species of cod, for fertiliser and were in the process of carting a load of the fish to their farms when the storm blew up. They dumped their load in their haste to reach shelter before the storm.   *(23)*

January, 1927

It is not uncommon for birds to catch fish. For example, the kingfisher, various wild ducks, and even the American bald eagle, all enjoy this pursuit. It is far less common, however, for fish to catch birds. But this does happen. The angler fish, common in European waters, has frequently been known to catch and swallow whole at least two different types of birds – puffins, or sea-parrots, and also trottellumes. These are fairly large birds. The sea-parrot can dive more than 100 feet deep and stay under water for up to three minutes. During these dives, it sometimes falls prey to the angler fish.   *(24)*

August, 1927

There have not been very many individuals who deliberately set out to cultivate the friendship of fishes. One man who did was Mr Armstrong Perry and, according to reports that were published in U.S.A. in August, 1927, he succeeded quite well in gaining the confidence of his finny friends.

Mr Perry took his project very seriously. He referred to his contacts with the fish world as "research in piscatorial sociology".

The project began when, in a dry season, Mr Perry established contacts with trout by gathering up those that had been left in shallow pools in a vanished stream and carrying them to larger waterholes where they had a chance to survive. He found that the fish sensed his helpful motive and he was able to catch them quite easily.

Another time, he established a friendship with 40 sunfish. They would meet him at the water's edge and accept worms from his fingers.

Carp became so trusting after having been fed bread by Mr Perry that they would let him lift them from the water.

Once, Mr Perry carried a catfish in his pocket until it was dry and appeared to be dead. But, when he placed it in water it revived and began swimming about again with its customary vigour. *(25)*

September, 1928

On 4 September, 1928, swimmers were driven out of the surf at Lavalette, New Jersey, by a solid mass of weakfish which charged at the beach. People screamed and panicked, several bathers were nearly drowned, and scores of people, including women and children, had to be rescued by life guards and passers-by. The weakfish were part of a massive school which extended three miles out to sea. So powerful was the force of the onrushing mass of fish that many people were literally hurled onto the beach.

The cause of this unusual occurrence was an attack on the weakfish by schools of bluefish. The panic-stricken weakfish turned and charged, seeking safety in the shallow water at the edge of the beach. Hundreds of weakfish were killed in their struggle to escape from the predators. *(26)*

October, 1928

An even stranger occurrence of this type was reported a few weeks later. This time, however, the headlong rush of fish to the shore was caused by some inexplicable, suicidal urge on the part of the fish.

For several days, toward the end of October, 1928, campfires dotted the Rockaway beaches as thousands of people "fished" merely by picking up fish from the beaches. The fish they were gathering were frost fish, a species which, for some unknown reason, charges at the shore, with the first frost of winter, by the light of the moon.

Not only did the frost fish kill themselves in countless numbers, they also carried to the beach in front of them millions of spearing, a small minnow-like, salt water fish. The latter were just unfortunate enough to be in the frost fishes' path. None of the fish-gatherers bothered to collect the spearings.

On the first night, when the suicide rush began, people strolling on the beach could hardly believe their eyes as millions of fish, shimmering like silver in the light of the moon, forced their way forward onto the sand. In some places they lay in piles six inches deep.   (27)

February, 1929

A swordfish and a shark were caught together on the one line by Mr S. Ellis at Whangaroa, New Zealand, in February, 1929. The swordfish was hooked first, then the shark began to attack it. Again and again the shark bit at the swordfish, almost severing its tail. But, during the melee, which lasted about 20 minutes, the shark got itself entangled in the line. Mr Ellis harpooned the shark, gaffed the swordfish and brought them both ashore.   (28)

August, 1930

When Mr and Mrs Ed Pascoe were the sole owners of a fishing resort at Lake Genevieve, near Freemont, Nebraska, in the 1920's and 1930's, they were able to drum up fish from the depths of the lake at will. This was attested to by numerous reliable witnesses. Not that the Pascoes had any supernatural ability. It had all been a matter of training.

The couple began to train the fish when they first took over the resort in 1925. When they threw food scraps into the lake they would bang a dishpan and whistle. The fish quickly learned to associate these sounds with food and soon they would come at the signal.

The Pascoes did regular demonstrations for their guests. They would go to the shore, whistle and thump the dishpan and in no time there would be fish swarming in the water by the hundred – bluegills, crappies and bullheads.

There was a catch though. Guests were not allowed to fish at that point. They had to go out into the lake and depend on their own luck and skill. The Pascoes felt that it would not be ethical to use their ability to call up the fish in order to make it easier for the fishermen. They considered that this would be a betrayal of the trust that the fish had learnt to place in them.

The guests did not mind. Even if they went home with empty baskets, they reckoned it was the worth the cost of the visit to have seen the fish answering the call to dinner.   *(29)*

November, 1930

George Morris, of Moonah, Tasmania, Australia, returned from a fishing trip with a story of having been attacked, and bitten, by a sea monster. Not only did he have a witness to the story, he was able to show deep teeth marks in his leg.

Morris and his companion, Charles Speed, were fishing from a small boat near the shore at East Risdon when the monster suddenly rose up out of the water and placed its forepaws on the gunwale. It then gripped Morris's leg with its teeth and hauled him overboard into the water. Morris was dragged a few yards but, with his free leg, he kicked the monster in the eye and this enabled him to escape and swim back to the boat where his friend helped him clamber aboard.

From the descriptions given by the two men, fishermen concluded that Morris had been attacked by a sea lion.   (30)

March, 1932

Mrs J. Kiser, of Norman Park, Georgia, was fishing in a pond when she hooked a small perch. It was so small she left it on the hook and laid down the pole for a moment, with the perch still in the water.

Next moment, the pole shot out into the pond. Mrs Kiser got into a boat and rowed out to retrieve her gear. When she reached the pole she found that she had, not one fish, but three! A small trout had swallowed the perch, hook and all, but then it, in turn, had been attacked by a larger trout, which was later found to weigh 5 pounds. The small trout was too big for the large one's mouth and held it as firmly as a hook would have done.   (31)

April, 1932

From Wildwood, New Jersey, came the report that a mackerel had been caught with a rubber band around its body. Captain Frank Favaora was the man who landed the fish and all he could suggest by way of explanation was that, while still a little fellow, the mackerel may have been nosing about in the mud when he stuck his head through the rubber band. It gripped tight and expanded gradually as the fish grew.   (32)

April, 1932

Hundreds of holiday-makers at Le Lavandou, a resort near Toulon, France, were horrified to witness a desperate struggle to save a five-year-old boy from the tentacles of a giant octopus. The octopus had been captured during the day by local fishermen and was being exhibited in a tank when the boy, not realising the danger, put his hand into the water.

The octopus immediately grabbed the boy around the wrist with its tentacles and commenced to drag him under the water. He was grabbed by those nearest to him and a tug-of-war ensued in which the octopus was more than holding his own. Then, when it seemed the boy was lost, a fisherman began slashing at the tentacles with his knife until the octopus sank to the bottom of the tank.

(33)

December, 1932

Reverend F. Browning, of the Melanesian Mission, had some interesting stories to tell when he returned to Sydney, Australia, after having spent eight years at Siota, in the Solomon Islands.

Mr Browning said that shark and crocodile flesh was highly prized in the Solomons as food and the islanders showed great daring in capturing these animals. Sharks were often seen sleeping, half submerged, in the waters about the islands and this gave the hunters an opportunity to employ their favourite tactic.

A native would gently ease himself into the water, carrying a rope in one hand, and slowly and cautiously swim towards the unsuspecting shark. The swimmer, and also his companions on the shore, would maintain absolute silence for the slightest splash or other noise would be enough to awaken their quarry.

Usually, the native would be successful in reaching the shark while it was still asleep and he would slip a noose over its tail, pull it tight and then swim as fast as he was able to the shore. At the same time, the shore party would haul on the rope and pull the shark in the opposite direction to that taken by the swimmer.

With luck, the swimmer would make it to safety and the shark would be hauled onto the beach and killed. Sometimes the shark would be the victor, of course, and there was a steady attrition of hunters, but the natives were philosophical about this risk.

A similar technique was used to capture crocodiles except that in this case the rope would be looped around the crocodile's legs.

The natives considered crocodile-hunting to be a less dangerous pursuit. They told Mr Browning that the reptiles were so lethargic during the day that they were usually quite easy to capture. Nevertheless, there were many stories about hunters suffering death or injury from these monsters.

One factor which operated in the hunter's favour was that a crocodile will rarely snap off an arm or leg from a human victim. He is quite capable of doing this with his powerful jaws and fearsome array of teeth. But that is not the crocodile's way. He prefers to get a good grip on his prey, kill it by drowning, then carry it off to his lair. Here, it is placed in his larder, left to putrefy and eaten at leisure.

For this reason, many natives have survived encounters with crocodiles. Some escaped by thrusting their fingers into the crocodile's eyes. One old man was famous among the islanders for his exploit in seizing a crocodile by the tongue during a fierce fight. *(34)*

May, 1933

Mr Charles Blanch, of Coffs Harbour, Australia, had a frightening, but at the same time very fortuitous, experience whilst fishing from a small boat. He was some distance out from the shore, and quite relaxed, he said, when a shadow fell across his boat. Then he realised that it was a large fish flying through the air. It was a monster mackerel weighing 40 pounds and it landed right in his boat. *(35)*

October, 1933

In an address to the Aquarium Society at the American Museum of Natural History, Mrs Horst von der Goltz told of a species of fish which not only showed clear signs of intelligence but also demonstrated an almost human capacity to care for its young.

Mrs von der Goltz said that her many years' observation of many types of fish had convinced her that all fish have some degree of intelligence but it does vary enormously with the species.

The least intelligent fish are those that live in schools. They are "dumb" compared with fish that live their own individual lives. The fish in schools are controlled by mob action and the individual does not do his own thinking.

In Mrs von der Goltz's experience, the most intelligent fish are cichlids, which are found in South America, Africa, India and Madagascar. They range in size from 2 inches to 10 inches.

The most outstanding thing about cichlids is the tender, loving care that they exhibit towards their young. They teach them to swim, wash them, feed them, put them to bed at sundown and wake them up for breakfast. They break their food up into small chunks and teach them to take care of themselves. The period of parental care lasts for three to four months.

The adult fish adopt a kind of Charlie Chaplin pantomime routine in their efforts to teach the young fish to beware of dangerous big fish. The pairs of adults live a monogamous life style, at least in captivity.

Each day, just before nightfall, the young would be put to bed in a sand-hole nest. Just for an experiment, Mrs von der Goltz put the tank in a dark room and turned the lights on at 10 o'clock in the morning and off at 10 o'clock in the evening. The fish parents soon slipped into the new routine. They would begin rounding up the young fish at 9.30 p.m., half an hour before bed-time.   (36)

December, 1934

Why the shark did it, no one knows, but two Australian fishermen at Sandgate, Queensland, found themselves in a desperate plight when a 20-foot shark seized their 15-pound anchor in its jaws and immediately dived deep. The bows of the fishing boat were dragged downwards and it was all the two men could do to stop the craft from capsizing.

While one man manipulated the tiller, in an attempt to keep the boat on an even keel, the other grabbed a knife and slashed at the anchor rope. He managed to sever the rope and sacrifice the anchor before they were dragged under water. *(37)*

April, 1935

Fish habits are based on memories of the species which go far back into the past, explained a French scientist, M. Le Danois, during a lecture delivered by him in Copenhagen. M. Le Danois was the head of the Parisian Scientific and Technical Bureau of Deep-Sea Fisheries and he had studied fish life in the northern seas for many years.

For example, some species of fish like the tunny are unaware of the existence of the English Channel, a feature which was scoured out of the landform by the sea during recent times, geologically speaking. As a result, when the tunny heads for the Baltic and North Sea, it follows a course west of the British Isles, just as its forbears did 100,000 years ago.

A good spot to catch herring, said M. Le Danois, is the spot which used to be at the mouth of the Rhine 100,000 years ago. The Rhine has retreated southward but the herring continue to breed at the traditional river mouth, rather than at its current position.

Scientists have found it possible to trace many prehistoric coastlines and riverbeds by studying the habits of fish. *(38)*

April, 1935

Staff Captain Stanley W. Moughtin of the Cunard White Star liner, *Carinthia*, had a story to tell whilst in New York in April, 1935 but he was a bit hesitant about whether he should do so. He did not want to get a reputation, he said, as a teller of tall tales, and this one was a bit hard to believe.

"Actually, it is not my story," said Captain Moughtin. "It was told to me by a passenger, so I can only tell it to you exactly as it was told to me."

"Late one afternoon, a Portuguese fisherman of the Bahamas, named Punkadilla, was out in his auxiliary schooner a few miles off Nassau when he sighted an enormous shark floating motionless on the surface of the sea. Punkadilla went close alongside and found that the marine man-eating monster was dead. He decided that it would be worthwhile to tow the great fish to Nassau and ground the carcase somewhere along the sandy shore away from the town.

"The fisherman," the passenger continued, "arrived after dark and grounded the shark in shallow water and ran a kedge anchor out so it would not drift away in the night.

"When Punkadilla reported the finding of the sea monster to one of the professors attached to the museum and aquarium, the professor drove out to see it and found that the shark was 63 feet long, 22 feet in beam and 12 feet deep down from the top fin, just about big enough to swim through the channel between the Bahama islands without grounding.

"The professor went back to town to procure saws, axes and large knives to open up the fish to see what it had died from. By its size it looked like dropsy.

"When the naturalist returned and, with the aid of the fisherman, Punkadilla, cut a hole in the side and entered the body of the shark, he found a large keg of oil, which had no doubt caused its death. The professor said the oil was seeping from the bung and apparently the shark had tasted the liquid when it was hungry and swallowed the keg, which could not be digested.

"The venerable professor, who seemed quite distressed over the agony endured by the shark, said the oil had no doubt made the big fish bilious and also so buoyant that it could not dive below the surface to search for food. The mishap had evidently caused the marine monster great pain, as its eyes showed traces of continuous tears.

"When the passenger got the first news of the finding of the shark, he said he drove over to the beach and found that the professor had opened the giant mouth and propped up the roof with its four rows of sharp pointed teeth with a bamboo pole so that he was able to walk inside without stooping.

"Moving pictures and photographs were to have been taken next morning, but unfortunately a howling northeaster blew up with heavy seas that washed the carcase out to sea.

"Of course, I did not see Punkadilla, the fisherman, or the aged professor," said Captain Moughtin, "but I will investigate the story this time at Nassau. I have seen enormous sharks in the Red Sea off Jeddah during the Mecca pilgrimage season, and at Muscat in the Persian Gulf, but I do not remember any that were quite 63 feet long." *(39)*

May, 1935

Wandering along a river bank in the Burragorang Valley, Australia, Mr C.G. Christie was fortunate enough to witness a most strange and interesting series of events. It began when he saw a bush-rat clambering out of the water with a small trout in its jaws. The rat lost no time in killing and eating his prey; then he climbed into the branches of a bush overhanging the water, and took up a vigil.

Enthralled by the spectacle, Mr Christie stood quietly and watched the drama for some considerable time. The rat sat patiently, his beady eyes scanning the gently flowing stream beneath him. Then, suddenly, he leaped into the water and emerged with another fish gripped between his teeth. By the time he finished his meal only the bones and head remained.

One would think that his hunger would have been sated by now, but, no. He took up his post again.

The next prospective victim was spotted well out into the stream in shallow water and the rat leaped down from his perch, jumped from rock to rock for part of the way, then swam the remaining distance, arriving in quick time at a spot just downstream from his quarry.

He approached the fish stealthily and, when about a foot away, he leaped. This time, however, the rat was not successful in his quest. The trout wriggled and plunged about desperately until it managed to reach deep water and quickly disappeared.

The disappointed rat made his way back to the bank where he resumed his vigil in the bush.   *(40)*

June, 1935

A traveller to what was then the Dutch East Indies (now Indonesia) returned with a weird story about a vendetta by a shark. He said that the seamen in that part of the world believed that if they were destined to die in the sea, then it would inevitably happen and nothing could be done to prevent it. They also believed, in accordance with traditions that had been passed down to them from time immemorial, that certain man-killing sea animals, once they formed a dislike for a particular man, would mark him for death and hunt him all their lives.

As proof that there is justification for this belief, the seamen tell the story of a swimmer who was attacked by a shark in the surf. The man carried a knife and was able to fight off the shark. Wounded during the attack, the shark followed the man toward the shore and hovered around vengefully for several hours.

One year later, at a beach many miles away, the man was rowing offshore when the boat was attacked by a large shark. The monster very nearly capsized the boat but the man dealt it some heavy blows with an oar and eventually drove it away. "It was the same shark," he said later. "I could tell by a big greenish blotch on its side, apparently an old scar."

Some months later the shark attacked the man for a third time while he was swimming with some friends. This time the shark was successful in killing his enemy.   *(41)*

August, 1935

Not fish, but frogs, are the central characters in this next story – and a very talented group of frogs they were, apparently. They were able to dive into water from a height of 75 feet without suffering any injury. This unusual ability was demonstrated at the site of an archaeological investigation of a Roman shaft at Ipswich, U.K.

The story about the frogs was told by Mr J. Reid Moir, who was engaged in the investigation. Mr Moir explained that the sides of the shaft were timbered and supported by cross-struts, while the water at the bottom was 75 feet from the surface, and confined in a metal caisson about 7 feet in diameter.

"It will be realised, therefore," he said "that it is no easy matter for any falling object to avoid hitting one of the cross-struts in its descent – or to strike the limited area of water inside the caisson. Yet this feat is accomplished nightly by frogs. Every morning several of these creatures are found swimming happily, and, as the work of excavation would speedily bring their careers to an end, they are carefully collected in a tin and conveyed to the surface.

"Now, while it may seem incredible that frogs should dive about 75 feet into water, there would seem no escape from this conclusion. They are certainly not coming into the excavation from the water pouring out of a fissure in the chalk, while, in no circumstances could they climb down the vertical timbering of the shaft. Moreover, one small frog was found the other day sitting in the large bucket which was suspended some little distance from the bottom, and this creature could only have reached its position from above.

"So far no frog has been found in any way damaged by its descent, but exactly how the trick is done passes my comprehension. I am tempted to spend a night at the excavation with a flashlamp in order to see this high-diving in progress." *(42)*

October, 1935

Harrison Outerbridge, of Bermuda, was trying to get the hang of fishing from a boat with a rod, when he struck a bit of trouble. He hooked a bonito but the fish pulled him overboard. Outerbridge kept his grip on the rod and swam back to the boat, pulling the fish behind him. But, as he scrambled back on board his boat, the fish jerked the rod from his grasp and took off again.

Outerbridge, still determined to win, dived overboard, retrieved the rod, and swam back to the boat. This time, he managed to get his prize aboard. He was somewhat crestfallen to find that the fish which had given him such a mighty battle, weighed only 5 pounds. *(43)*

August, 1937

An interesting incident was witnessed by Zeke Simpkins whilst casting for bass in the Salamonie River, Indiana. A sparrow alighted on some floating debris and, almost immediately, a black snake struck at it and began to swallow it. Next moment, a bass struck at the snake's tail. The snake spun round, startled, and the sparrow escaped. *(44)*

August, 1937

A native named Iona, diving for pearls near Thursday Island, to the north of Australia, had a miraculous escape from death when his head was seized by a 10-foot shark. He jammed his thumbs into the shark's eyes and forced it to relinquish its grip on him.

Iona was in shallow water, only about twelve feet deep, when he was attacked. As soon as he broke free from the shark, he shot to the surface and was pulled aboard the lugger.

It took a doctor two hours to stitch up the wounds in Iona's face, neck and chest. There were two rows of teeth marks and they required almost 200 stitches.

This was the second time that a diver survived such a predicament in these waters. Some years previously, another native named Treacle found his head inside a shark's mouth and he freed himself by the same method. *(45)*

December, 1937

Three Darwin men, whilst on a week-end crocodile-shooting expedition near the mouth of the Adelaide River, Australia, witnessed a fight to the death between a shark and a crocodile.

The men were in an aboriginal dugout canoe, paddling down the river with the tide, and were shooting at crocodiles on the banks. They were about to shoot at a 10-foot crocodile they had spotted lying at the junction of a small creek with the river when, suddenly, the crocodile began to thresh the water with its tail and a 7-foot shark was flung into the air.

The crocodile swung round and dived. The water was beaten into foam as the two monsters battled beneath the surface. The crocodile surfaced, attempting to drag the shark onto a mudflat but the shark was still very much alive and another fierce fight was commenced. Soon, attempts were made by the badly-mauled shark to escape, but it was too late, and as its struggles gradually ceased, the observers saw its bloodstained fin above the surface as it was dragged into the creek mouth, defeated. *(46)*

April, 1938

Dr Christopher W. Coates, of the New York Aquarium, told newspaper reporters an interesting story which involved electric eels, rats and cats.

The Aquarium had been experiencing problems with rats, great hulking brutes which were believed to have scurried off ships that were tied up nearby. In the winter the rats were particularly bad. They would balance on the tank tops and scoop out of the water any small fish which were unwary enough to approach the surface of the water.

Occasionally, a rat would lose its balance, fall into the water and be drowned. But this did not happen often enough. The attrition rate among the fish was still much too high.

The Aquarium therefore acquired four cats which it hoped would keep the rats in check. But, the plan was not 100% successful because cats also like fish and Dr Coates soon found that they were putting much more effort into fishing than they were into killing rats.

Drastic measures were needed; and this was where the electric eels came into the story. Dr Coates removed several electric eels from their tanks, each of the wriggly animals being about 5 feet in length, and placed them on the floor. (This caused the eels no problem because they can live for an hour or two out of the water.)

Then he released the cats and sat back to watch the fun. The cats, smelling fresh meat, promptly advanced to investigate. In a way, they were lucky, for they only received mild electric shocks of about ten volts or so. If one of them had touched an eel's head and tail at the same time, it would have been the end of the cat because it would have received a charge of 500 volts – enough to knock down a horse.

After a few such experiments, the cats lost interest in all aquatic creatures, including fish, and gave their full attention to the rats. So the Aquarium's problem was solved.   (47)

April, 1938

In a lecture delivered to the members of three scientific and technical organisations, Dr Christopher W. Coates, of the New York Aquarium, said that the ancient Indians of South America were the first to experiment with electricity in the treatment of rheumatism. For this purpose, they applied electric eels to the bodies of rheumatics.

Later, white people in South America heard about this odd treatment, but they misunderstood the technique. They ate the

122

eels. Apparently, the flesh was not very tasty because one guinea pig, after eating a dish of eels, said that he would rather put up with the rheumatism. *(48)*

May, 1938

Do fish like music? And if so, what kind of music do they like? These questions were fiercely debated between fishermen, as well as scientists, when Dr Maurice Klein presented the results of his two years' research.

Dr Klein, physician and research physicist, a retired Newark eye and ear specialist, argued that some musical vibrations have a definite attraction for fish. The doctor invited skeptics to examine his thesis, entitled "The Stimulating and Depressive Influence of Musical Vibrations on Ichthyopsida".

Dr Klein began his experiments at Ashbury Park, New Jersey, in 1936 when he noticed that musical vibrations transmitted from the Convention Hall organ through the steel and concrete caissons on which the building extends seaward had a definite effect on fish in the vicinity.

Intrigued by the discovery, Dr Klein obtained the cooperation of G. Howard Scott, municipal organist, and the two men conducted a series of tests. They found that the vibrations extend through the water in a fan-shaped pattern and that the soothing harmonies of old masters like Schubert attracted fish towards the shore. On the other hand, when the organist launched into "swing" music, the "sudden, violent noises" caused the fish to go scurrying out to sea.

The theoretical arguments raged back and forth for some weeks and were somewhat inconclusive, but one keen fisherman, Mr H. Nemetz, who put Dr Klein's theories to a practical test, could not have been happier with the results.

Mr Nemetz took his portable phonograph with him when he went fishing and played records of Bach's *Passacaglia in C minor* and

Beethoven's *Sonata Pathetique*. His success was phenomenal! The waters were alive with fish. Then, for experimental purposes only, he played some swing music – a record called *I've Got Ants in My Pants*. Straight away, the fish disappeared. *(49-50)*

May, 1938

Charlie, the educated bass, and his human friend, Captain Harold Thomas, became quite famous around Saranac Lake, New York, in the late 1930's.

Captain Thomas would blow a whistle and, in response, Charlie would emerge from beneath the dock, swim to the surface and accept a choice crawfish from the captain's fingers.

Some newspaper reporters expressed skepticism regarding Captain Thomas's claim that Charlie would allow the captain to remove him from the water, weigh him, and return him to his natural element without Charlie's calm being upset in the slightest. At Captain Thomas's invitation, the reporters watched, amazed, while he did exactly that. *(51)*

July, 1938

When a brown cattle dog began barking excitedly at the end of a pier at Queenscliff, Australia, a number of fishermen went to investigate. What had attracted the dog's attention was a whip-tailed shark, 4 feet long, which was swimming on the surface.

As the men arrived, the dog suddenly jumped into the water, seized the shark and swam with it about 40 yards to the landing. The men lifted the shark from the water and found that, although it was still alive, it was cut about the throat from the dog's teeth.

The whip-tailed shark gets its name from the fact that it kills its prey with its tail. *(52)*

August, 1938

An astonished observer, Mrs H.W. Bryan, of St. Petersburg, Florida, saw a spider catch a 3-inch goldfish in a lily pond. The spider, about a half-dollar in size, clung to a lily pad, held the fish's mouth and gills above the water until it died, then ate it.   *(53)*

April, 1939

A few decades back, it became a popular, if strange fad, particularly among university students, to swallow live goldfish.

Claude C. Curtis, an employee at the Grassyfork Hatcheries, Indiana, performed a hard-to-beat feat in this category when he swallowed a cup of water in which 5,000 young fish were swimming around.   They were so tiny that they were barely visible.   *(54)*

July, 1939

While fly-casting at Highland Lake, near Winsted, Conn., Hugh Meade, the Torrington Chief of Police, observed a pickerel which was just about to seize his lure.   But, just then, Meade's gold watch slipped from his wrist into the water.   The pickerel turned away from the fly, swallowed the watch and swam away.   *(55)*

August, 1939

Three dogs battled with a shark which attacked them in Northwest Creek, L.I., while they were being put through a training exercise.   The dogs, all golden retrievers, were pursuing imitation ducks when an 8-foot sand shark came upon the scene.

Philip Collins, the dogs' trainer, was on the shore watching when he saw a terrible commotion in the water.   He rowed out to the scene and found that one dog, Golden Dawn, was attacking the shark's head.   The other two dogs were trying to sink their teeth into the shark's tail, but without much success for its hide was too tough. Collins bashed the shark's head with the anchor and this put it to flight.   The only casualty was Golden Dawn, who suffered many lacerations from the shark's teeth. Twelve stitches were required to close the dog's wounds.   *(56)*

August, 1939

Peter, a pike owned by a Britisher, Mr Clifford Bower-Shore, regularly showed his master that he had at least some degree of intelligence. It was Mr Bower-Shore's practice to feed the fish with worms that he found in his garden and Peter obviously appreciated these little delicacies. The fish soon came to realise that the worms were always tipped into his tank from a particular small, shiny tin. When Mr Bower-Shore walked into the room without this tin in his hand, Peter would ignore his presence. But if his master had that shiny tin in his hand, Peter would bob about the water with his nose expectantly at the surface.

So, not only do people like to watch fish swimming around in their tank; apparently the fish also keep an eye on people, to see what they are up to. *(57)*

Fish Bait

Fishermen often argue about the respective merits of various kinds of bait; but perhaps the kind of bait you use is not all that important after all. Don McLaughlin, of Binghamton, New York, used a raw potato for bait when he caught a 13-pound carp in the Chenango River. *(58)*

Whilst on the subject of bait, if you want to catch really big fish perhaps you should use the giant Gippsland earthworm – the world's largest – which is found in south-eastern Victoria, Australia. This species grows to more than 6 feet in length and is as thick as a man's thumb. They are not difficult to find because they make a distinct gurgling sound as they burrow through the ground. *(59)*

On the other hand, if you want to confuse the fish, you could use the Pennsylvania jumping worm which has a head at each end. Great excitement was generated in Susquehanna, Pa., in the 1930's when a number of these worms were found and one was placed on exhibition in a hardware store.

About 6 inches long and as thick as a pencil, the exhibition worm fascinated hundreds of people as it raised its heads, one at a time, moved backwards and forwards on its numerous legs and, at one stage, flipped over on its back as someone tried to touch it. It also demonstrated an ability to jump about an inch into the air, hence its name.

A local newspaper editor examined one of the worms with a magnifying glass. He said that at one end there was a head with two small eyes, surrounded by whiskers. At the other end was a head without whiskers but with one large eye – about as big as a match head. The worm was able to move backward or forward with equal ease on 30 tiny feet.   *(60)*

September, 1939

James Sparkman, of Hot Springs, Ark., reported that his cow, Sally, caught a 6-pound bass with her tail. She waded into a shallow pond, seeking relief from the heat, when suddenly she bellowed noisily and lumbered back onto dry ground. Dangling from her tail was the fish, with its teeth firmly enmeshed in the hairs on Sally's tail.   *(61)*

October, 1939

At Reading, Pa., a resident, George Stofflet, was standing idly on his front porch when a 12-inch trout landed at his feet – already cooked. A heron had been flying overhead, carrying the trout, but the fish had managed to wriggle free. During its fall, it struck high tension wires, then bounced off and landed in front of Stofflet's house. Mr Stofflet proudly displayed a picture of himself holding the fish, which had been fried in an instant by 66,000 volts.   *(62)*

December, 1940

A friendly English trout attached itself to the Leeder family of Healesville, Victoria, Australia, and, up to the time of the report in 1940, had remained faithful to them for more than five years. It would come when called by Mrs Alf Leeder and would take raw meat and other food scraps from her hand.

The trout lived in the Graceburn River, close to the Leeder's home. Anglers had often tried to catch it but none succeeded. Mrs Leeder said that they had no chance of capturing it because it was large, fat and so well fed that it was not the slightest bit interested in any food attached to a line. *(63)*

June, 1941

Five attendants at the New York Aquarium made an unsuccessful attempt to weigh a Blitzkrieg fish, also known as the torpedo ray. This fish is capable of producing an electrical discharge of more than 200 volts and a power output of about 3 horsepower in a fraction of a second.

The fish was 4 feet long, over 2 feet wide and was estimated to weigh between 40 and 50 pounds. Its exact weight was not determined because it delivered a heavy discharge of electricity just as the five attendants were about to weigh it. The attendants were momentarily paralysed and, as soon as they recovered, they dropped it into its tank without further delay. *(64)*

September, 1941

Several dozen goldfish were taught to swim a maze by John W. French, a researcher at Princeton University. Mr French explained the techniques used in the experiment to members of the American Psychological Association.

Goldfish do not like to be subjected to strong light so the maze consisted of a series of tunnels, all brightly lit, with several blind alleys and only one proper exit. The correct exit led into a shaded chamber which the goldfish found more to its liking. If it reached this chamber, the goldfish was given a tit-bit of food as an added inducement.

According to the rules of the experiment, a fish was allowed to poke its nose into a blind alley, but if it went in far enough to admit any part of its tail, this was considered to be an error.

After completing 30 tries, each one taking about four minutes, it was found that the fish had learned the maze so well that they were able to complete the run successfully five times without an error.   *(65)*

October, 1941

Even fish, it seems, can find solace in alcohol. One fish even learned to go on a daily alcoholic bender. The story was told by Homer M. Green, of Middletown, New York. While fishing in one of his privately-stocked ponds, Mr Green landed a sunfish. He considered it too small to keep, but before throwing it back he noticed that its mouth was badly lacerated and he decided to give it some quick first aid treatment. The only thing he had handy which would serve the purpose was a bottle of apple-jack (apple brandy) so he poured some of this liquid on the lacerations.

Next day, and, every day from then on when Mr Green was fishing at the same spot, that same fish would present himself for the first aid treatment. On receiving it, he would do numerous flip-flops in the air.   *(66)*

November, 1945

A live fish one inch long was found in the white of a normal-sized egg laid by a hen in Liverpool, U.K. The most plausible explanation to the mystery was that the fish came from spawn germinated from fish meal, which had been part of the hen's diet.   *(67)*

August, 1947

A Malay villager was taken to hospital in a very distressed condition after a fish jumped down his throat. The Malay had been fishing with a net and was peering over the edge of it to inspect his catch when the accident occurred.

Dr R.M.B. Lowis, who treated the victim, said that the spiked fin of the fish had embedded itself in the pharyngeal wall. He initially attempted to remove the fish with sponge-holding forceps but the tail came off. The fish was finally removed in the operating theatre and the patient made a good recovery.

The fish was found to be an Ikan Betok, 6 inches long and 4 inches in circumference at the thickest part its body. *(68)*

Jonah and the Whale

We all know the story of Jonah and the whale but is it really possible for a person to be swallowed by a whale and survive? According to *Stranger Than Science* by Frank Edwards, there is a well-documented case where this actually happened. Edwards claims that the official records of the British Admiralty provide documentary evidence for the astounding occurrence.

The unfortunate, or fortunate man – whichever you like to call him – was James Bartley, a 21-year-old British seaman, who served on the whaling ship *Star of the East* in 1891. When a huge sperm whale was sighted by the lookout, three boats set off after it, Bartley being among the crew of one of them. As it happened, Bartley's boat was the first to reach the whale and the harpooner drove his harpoon deep into its body. They then backed off fast as the stricken beast began to thresh the water with its giant tail.

The whale dived and 800 feet of the heavy line attached to the harpoon streaked down into the depths of the ocean. Then the line ceased to uncoil and there was a long, quiet pause as the sailors sat, gripping their oars, waiting to see what the whale would do next.

They did not have long to wait. The wounded whale came up right underneath them and tossed their boat into the air.

The other two boats came in and picked up all the survivors they could find but two men were missing, one of whom was James Bartley.

Later that day the dying whale floated to the surface and the men winched it to the ship and began cutting it up. At 11 o'clock that night, working by lantern light, they noticed a movement in the whale's stomach, cut it open and found James Bartley, unconscious but still alive.

The ship's doctor had Bartley drenched with buckets of sea water. This had the desired effect of reviving him but when he regained consciousness, he was completely out of his mind and babbled incoherently for almost two weeks. Then he gradually recovered his senses and was able to tell what he remembered about his experience. He could recollect being flung into the air, landing in the enormous mouth and sliding down a slimy tube. He remembered struggling for breath, then, oblivion.

Bartley was inside the whale for 15 hours and the whale's gastric juices affected his body severely. All the hair had disappeared from his body, his skin had been bleached to an unnatural whiteness and his sight was greatly weakened.

He returned to Gloucester where he lived for a further 18 years. When he died, his tombstone was inscribed with a brief account of his terrible experience and a footnote which states: "James Bartley: 1870-1909 ... a modern Jonah."   *(69)*

The fate of another man who was swallowed by a sperm whale was told in a letter published in the June, 1947 issue of *Natural History Magazine* from Dr Egerton Y. Davis, of Boston. Dr Davis was an eye-witness to the incident, which occurred during the 1890's while he was on board a sealing vessel.

"The whale was apparently as lost and out of season in those Arctic waters as he was confused and angered by the sudden appearance of a fleet of ships and men," wrote the doctor.

In full view of the crew of one of the ships, a sailor fell from an ice floe, landed close to a sperm whale and was somehow swallowed. The whale was killed shortly after and the men hacked their way into its carcase in an effort to recover their friend's body.

"When they recovered it," said the doctor, "the appearance and odor were so bad that all save I were forced to turn away, and we were obliged to consign him to the briny deep." *(70)*

Roy Chapman Andrews decided to carry out a practical test in regard to a whale's ability to swallow humans. In describing his experience, he said:

> So I pushed my body partly down the throat of a dead 60-foot sperm whale. I could just squeeze through. A fat man couldn't have made it. But of course a man would be dead long before he got into the stomach. *(71)*

March, 1948

We have mentioned elsewhere that the behaviour of the North Sea herring is strangely affected by the moon. It has also been discovered that oysters are subject to the moon's influence. A fishery expert at the Colonial Office, in the U.K., announced that a study had shown that oysters open their shells and begin to feed at the exact moment when the moon passes over the meridian in which they lie. *(72)*

September, 1948

A 13-year-old-boy, fishing with some of his friends from a coal pier at Botany Bay, Australia, caught a small octopus which held firmly in its tentacles an unexploded hand grenade.

The boy, Donald Smith, thought at first that the octopus was holding a stone. He and his friends were about to kill it with an iron bar when they realised the object was a hand grenade.

They then retreated about 50 yards down the pier. They saw the octopus drop the hand grenade, slither across the pier and return to the water.

Donald Smith then picked up the hand grenade and took it to Botany police station. Army authorities later examined it and said that the detonator and explosives would not have been affected by the grenade's immersion in water. They found that it was

complete with pin, lever and detonator, in other words, still a
lethal weapon. *(73)*

September, 1948

For many generations, fishermen from Lowestoft, England, knew
that the best catches of the year were available at the time of the
October full moon. Scientists never took the claim very seriously
until a study of 12 years' records proved that the fishermen were
right.

Further investigations revealed facts that the scientists found
quite astonishing. It seems that on the night of the full moon
nearest to October 11, the North Sea herring have a kind of fish
carnival during which they come to the surface, flip about like
mad, and completely ignore the fishermen's nets which scoop
them up by the million. Why they behave in this fashion is still a
mystery. *(74)*

October, 1948

Tiny fish have been observed swimming about in the artesian bore
water near Longreach, Queensland, Australia, although the water
is almost at boiling point. The water comes from deep down in
the bowels of the earth and, for some reason, the fish do not live
long after reaching the surface. They have eye sockets but no
eyes. *(75)*

November, 1948

Twenty-five families who lived in the eastern section of a
six-storey apartment house in the Bronx found one day that they
were without cold water. Residents living in the western section
still had their normal water supply so a plumber who was called
concluded that there was a blockage in the 2-inch pipe leading
from the basement to the eastern side of the building.

He cut the pipe and found that the problem had been caused by
an eel 39 inches in length. *(76)*

December, 1948

Guests staying at the Angler's Hotel at Durban, South Africa, witnessed an amazing fight between a hippopotamus and five sharks. The hippo was dozing lazily in St. Lucia Bay when the squadron of sharks cruised in and attacked it. The battle raged for ten minutes, during which the hippo put up a tremendous fight. It hurled four sharks completely out of the water, up onto the shore. Here, they were killed by people who had gathered to watch the fight. The fifth shark turned tail and swam back out to the open sea. *(77)*

February, 1949

The 1949 annual meeting of the American Institute of Electrical Engineers was treated to an unusual lecture and demonstration by Dr Christopher Coates, of the New York Aquarium. The subject was electric eels.

The 200 engineers who attended the meeting learned that one healthy electric eel is capable of generating 700 volts and one ampere – enough to light seven 100-watt bulbs.

"Dr Coates handled the eels with tender affection and rubber gloves," said one spectator. The largest eel was about 6 feet long and was considered by the audience to be one of the ugliest creatures they had ever seen.

"We have to be careful when we handle these animals," said Dr Coates. "Several animal collectors have been badly shocked whilst handling them carelessly."

Just at this point, one of the eels escaped from Dr Coates's grasp, began wriggling about near the feet of the engineers sitting in the front row,   and caused mild pandemonium until he was recaptured. *(78)*

September, 1949

One of the star attractions of the Commerce Department

Aquarium in Washington was "Superdiamond", the two-headed turtle. He lived for two years, to September, 1949, but he had a frustrating existence because his two heads could never agree on anything.

When one head wanted to sleep, the other would be wide awake. When one head, with some of the legs, would make for the door, the other head, with the remaining legs, would make for the window. As a result, Superdiamond rarely got to go anywhere. Despite the fact that all food eaten went to the same stomach, the two heads were never able to agree on which head saw a particular morsel of food first. Superdiamond's keepers felt that the turtle (turtles?) died from pure frustration. *(79)*

February, 1950

Mrs Lola Allison, of Broadmeadow, Australia, was bitten by a dead shark at the Newcastle Show. Mrs Allison's father was the proprietor of a side-show which featured man-eating sharks. She was trying to force open the jaws of a 7-foot grey nurse shark when the stick she was using broke and the shark's jaws snapped shut on her hand. She suffered deep puncture wounds to the right hand. *(80)*

April, 1950

Whilst fishing from the shore of the Red River in Wisconsin, Theodore Olecho of Chicago had some good luck and some bad luck. He hooked a big pike. The good luck was that it didn't get away. The bad luck was that the pike pulled Mr Olecho off his feet and he broke his leg. *(81)*

April, 1950

Edwin Forsythe, of Maine, dropped his false teeth overboard whilst building a weir. Four months later, he was rolling in his fishing net at the same spot when he found, tangled in the net, the missing teeth. *(82)*

April, 1950

Anglers at a brook near Ludlow, Mass., thought it strange that they should all have been so unlucky on the opening day of the trout season. But there was a reason, as Conservation Officer Whyte discovered. Somebody had sowed the pond liberally with hamburger to discourage the trout from biting. *(83)*

April, 1950

Mr C.M. Brooks, of Prarie du Chien, Wis., was able to assure his friends that the fish were really biting after he put his hand into the water to clear away some weeds. A black bass seized his finger and only let go when he pulled the fish half out of the water. *(84)*

136

April, 1950

A Burmese boy found himself in hospital, suffering terrible pain because he tried to bite a live fish. He was carrying water from a well when the fish nipped his finger. The boy was infuriated, grabbed hold of the fish and attempted to bite it, but the fish fought back. It jumped, wriggled and squirmed and finished up sliding down the boy's throat.

At last report, doctors were giving him medicine in an attempt to kill the fish. *(85)*

April, 1952

Over a period of about four years, William Ker, who lived in a remote bay in the Marlborough Sounds, South Island, New Zealand, became friends with about a hundred fish. Blue cod were the first fish to come when he began throwing food into the water and they were later followed by snapper. The snapper varied in size from about 6 pounds to 24 pounds.

Mr Ker hand-fed them every night and over the years they gradually became quieter and more trusting. He would stand in the water while the fish swam around him and they would raise their heads to take food. Eventually he was able to pick them up out of the water in his hands.

Many of the fish had been given names. There were two snapper, for instance, that he called Hector and Little Bella.

Tourists who returned from the sounds with this story were able to prove the truth of it with pictures. *(86)*

July, 1952

An interesting court action resulted from a dispute in a Paris restaurant. The trouble began when M. Magnieu complained to the restaurant proprietor that the lobsters offered to him were not fresh.

Waving his arms excitedly, the proprietor slapped down a basket full of lobsters on the table in front of the diner, took hold of the largest specimen and held it under the diner's nose, shouting, "My lobsters are all fresh – here, smell it!"

As if to prove the point, the lobster seized hold of M. Magnieu's nose with its claws and nipped out a small piece of flesh. M. Magnieu was awarded £100 damages. The restaurant proprietor's defence was that the lobster probably did not like the expression on the diner's face. *(87)*

October, 1953

To settle a wager, Colonel Esmond Drury, a 43-year-old sales manager, who was regarded as one of Britain's leading fly fishermen, cast a 2-ounce lead 105 yards from the roof of the Savoy Hotel into the Thames. The wager was between two anonymous hotel guests and had been made at a party held at the hotel during the previous month. Colonel Drury did not have any money on himself but he was rewarded with a free dinner for six people.

The colonel was dressed for the occasion in a brown cardigan and green corduroys. He strapped himself to a stanchion with a window cleaner's belt and was successful with his first cast.

He used a 10-foot 6-inch salmon rod and cast the lead high over the road – which the police had obligingly agreed to clear for the attempt – and over a tree which stood by the wall. The lead landed two yards into the Thames.

"Not bad, what?" was the colonel's comment. *(88)*

April, 1954

The United Nations announced an almost miraculous result of a fish-breeding experiment which was carried out in Thailand.

In February 1953 researchers placed 200 pairs of a species of fish called tilapia in an experimental pond half an acre in size and just over 4 feet deep.

One year later there were 134,700 tilapia in the pond. Most of the fish were distributed to farmers so that they could begin their own fish-breeding projects.

The scheme was organised by experts from the United Nations Food and Agricultural Organisation in cooperation with the staff of the local Fisheries Department. The object was to provide an additional source of protein for the population, as well as additional profit for the farmers. *(89)*

June, 1954

The captain of a fishing trawler from Liverpool, Nova Scotia, almost lost his life when a fish hook was driven through the bridge of his nose and he was hauled head-first towards the trawl winch. Only quick action by a member of his crew saved him. One of the men leapt to the winch and stopped it seconds before the captain would have been drawn face first into the meshing gears.

Captain Warren Levy, 41, had been standing by the rail of the trawler as a winch drew in the trawl line with its dozens of dangling hooks. One of the hooks flew up, gashed his forehead, then pierced the bridge of his nose.

The crew were forced to carry out some rough and ready surgery on the skipper. They ground off the eye of the hook with a coarse file, pulled the hook free, then poured iodine onto the wound.

In true sea captain tradition, Captain Levy then ordered the men back to work and refused to turn shoreward until the last trawl was hauled in.

Halifax Hospital reported that night that Captain Levy's condition was satisfactory. *(90)*

July, 1954

An angler, holidaying in Scotland, was saved from being washed down a river by the skill of a local champion golfer.

The angler began calling for help when he realised that he was trapped on a small island at Newton Stewart by the rapidly-rising river.

People who were nearby attempted to throw a rope to him, but without success. Then, along came Robbie Murray, champion golfer of the county of Wigtownshire. He tied a string to a golf ball, tied the other end of the string to the rope, then, without any difficulty, drove the golf ball across on to the island. The fisherman was then hauled ashore.   *(91)*

February, 1955

Mr Hubertus van Pel, the Fisheries Officer for the South Pacific Commission, announced that a team of Dutch scientists had found sharks and huge sawfish in a freshwater mountain lake 500 feet above sea level and 20 miles from the coast of what was then Dutch New Guinea (now Irian Jaya). How these salt-water sea monsters got up into the mountains and how they became acclimatised to fresh water is a mystery.

The beautiful mountain lake, called Sentani, is in the western part of the territory.

Mr van Pel said that the scientists were not able to name the variety of sharks. He said that one sawfish that had been caught was more than 10 feet long.

The only explanation the Dutch scientists could give was that the lake, thousands of years ago, was fed from the sea at sea level. Then a volcanic eruption took the lake 500 feet up when mountains rose out of the sea. The change from salt to fresh water was so gradual that the sharks and other habitual sea fish became acclimatised.   *(92)*

April, 1955

A 20-year-old man died whilst trying to kill fish with potassium cyanide at Turin, Italy. Giovanni Riva threw the poison into a canal. It was effective in killing the fish but Riva had a cut on his ankle and when he went into the water to retrieve the dead fish, the deadly poison entered his system. *(93)*

February, 1956

A priest was hit on the shoulder by a fish which fell from the sky during a rainstorm at North Sydney, Australia. Reverend Leonard Bourne was crossing the courtyard of St. Mary's Presbytery to attend mass when the fish struck him. It escaped in the flooded courtyard. Reverend Bourne had no idea what species of fish it was, but said it was about three inches long.

Commenting on the incident, Mr T.C. Roughley, former Director of New South Wales Fisheries, said, "It is very rare for a person to be hit with only one fish. Father Bourne is lucky he was not hit with a shoal of fish. The phenomenon is not unknown in country areas, but is less common on the coast. A circular wind like a willy-willy lifts up water from a pond or a dam, carries it through the air at a great speed and deposits it some distance away. It is not unusual for a shoal of small fish to be airborne in this manner." *(94)*

April, 1956

On April 21, 1956 the country town of Forbes, New South Wales, Australia, was showered with fish weighing up to a pound and a half each. But there was a logical, and obvious, explanation. The fish were dropped by hundreds of pelicans.

The birds had been raiding the fish in Lake Forbes but apparently their eyes were bigger than their bills. They dropped many of the fish in flight, most of them landing on the town's business centre. *(95)*

April, 1957

A man was heard calling for help at 2 o'clock in the morning, near the water's edge at Newcastle, Australia. The call was reported and a police launch raced across the bay to investigate.

141

The police soon found the man who needed help. His problem? He was holding on to three baited lines and, as he explained with a red face, he had caught three fish all at once. His call for help had been directed at a friend who was fishing nearby. *(96)*

May, 1957

A large shark that attacked Solomon Islander, Elison Sevo, of Ysabel Island, probably got the shock of his life. Sevo bit it back.

Sevo was spear-fishing, and having considerable success. He had speared one fish, put a string through its gills and tied the string around his waist. Then he speared another, bigger fish and was holding it when the shark attacked, savaging his leg and knee.

Sevo's response was to grab the shark, hold it against his chest and bite it on the nose and head until it was half dead. Then he fainted. He was dragged into a canoe by friends and taken ashore where his wounds were treated. *(97)*

December, 1958

An angler saved a three-year-old boy from drowning by hooking his jacket with an amazing 20-yard cast. The boy was given artificial respiration and admitted to hospital suffering from shock.

James Stansfield, 52, a retired newsagent, saw the boy, Robert Reid, being swept down the fast-flowing River Wyre, at Fleetwood, Lancashire. His first cast missed and the boy, who was floating face-down and unconscious, continued drifting with the current. The second cast landed the baited hook right on the boy's jacket and the angler reeled him in. *(98)*

August, 1959

The trawler, *Benfiquista*, limped into port at Caminha, Portugal, very lucky to have survived an attack by a frenzied giant swordfish. The skipper said he had swung the helm in vain attempts to evade the attack but the swordfish would not be denied. Its 5-foot spear pierced the ship's side but broke off in the middle at the time of impact.

When the trawler reached port, the crew were absolutely exhausted, having manned the pumps since the attack, which occurred early on the previous day. Nets and all other fishing gear had been flung overboard as they battled their way home through rough weather. *(99)*

September, 1959

It was a proud day for Allan Turton, aged 13, of Gymea Bay, Australia, when he landed a jewfish about as big as himself. The fish was 5 feet long, 3 inches taller than Allan, and, at 50 pounds, it was only 28 pounds lighter. *(100)*

1961, 1966 and 1983

Those strange stories about piranha fish eating people really are true. The fish are only tiny, but they are ferocious.

In April, 1961, newspapers around the world reported the story of a launch which sank in the Purus River, a northern tributary of the Amazon. A school of piranhas swept in and killed at least 10 people.

In February, 1966, seven children were eaten alive when their canoe capsized on a river in the east Peruvian jungle province of Madre de Dios. A fisherman who went to their aid suffered the same fate.

In May, 1983, when a canoe carrying 20 people overturned in the Madre de Dios River, five people were killed and the other 15 seriously injured by piranhas. *(101-103)*

December, 1962

Two fishermen from Poole, Dorset (U.K.), told how they saved the life of a cormorant which had been almost swallowed by an angler fish.

143

Sidney and John Hayes were about three miles offshore in their boat when they saw an object floating in the water. When they drew close to investigate, they found that it was a 3-foot long angler fish with a live cormorant clenched between its jaws.

Mr Sidney Hayes said, "By the time we had manoeuvred alongside, the fish had half swallowed the bird. Only the head and part of the wings were visible. But we managed to get a rope around it and to gradually pull it out, despite a terrific struggle by the fish, which we held with a boathook.

"It took us 20 minutes to get the cormorant free. With a couple of squawks it flew off, apparently none the worse for having been almost swallowed alive. But the angler fish just turned over on its side and floated away – it had choked to death. The fight must have started underwater when the cormorant dived down for food. The angler fish snapped at it and they fought their way up to the surface." *(104)*

1966

Richard Lurie reported an amusing incident which occurred on Australia's Great Barrier Reef. Whilst scuba diving, he came across two turtles fighting furiously and he waited, curious to see the outcome. The antagonists swooped, rolled and snapped at each other until one of the turtles happened to notice that they had a spectator. This knowledge disturbed his concentration and the other turtle began to get the upper hand.

The loser withdrew inside his shell but the victor continued to peck at his withdrawn head. He would not let up in his attack so Lurie decided he would take a hand in the matter. He swam up behind the winner, lifted his camera, and rapped hard on the turtle's shell.

Said Lurie, "If a male turtle was ever close to laying eggs, this was the time! When the self-satisfied head spun around, a look of incredulous surprise spread over its face. The eyes widened and the mouth opened ..." He then whirled around and sped off, accompanied by his adversary. *(105)*

On another occasion, and in the same area, Lurie witnessed an attack by some large fish on a number of sea birds. The birds had alighted on the still sea and were slowly paddling around when Lurie noticed a number of dorsal fins approaching rapidly towards them.

They were fish about 4 feet long which Lurie thought were probably ling or black kingfish. About 40 yards from the birds, the fins disappeared as the fish dived. Next moment, the head of one of the predators broke the surface and one of the sea birds was dragged down with a flurry of feathers. The remaining birds took off quickly enough to escape. *(106)*

March, 1967

A policeman, patrolling his beat at King's Lynn, Norfolk (U.K.), in the early hours of the morning, must have been quite sure that he was seeing things. Crawling down the street towards him were over 100 crabs. They were heading for the river.

Despite the crabs' determination to resist arrest, he managed to return them to the fishmonger's shop from which they had escaped. *(107)*

April, 1967

John Culshaw, aged 16, was fishing beside a bridge on the River Avon, at Hamilton (U.K.), when he unknowingly hooked a drowning 20-month-old baby boy. He thought at first that his line had fouled on an old jacket and began reeling his line in to free it by hand.

When he realised it was a baby on the line he shouted for help and the baby's father, Mr Samuel Rodger, ran into the water and brought the baby out. Mrs Rodger gave the baby the kiss of life for ten minutes before he revived. *(108)*

August, 1968

The Royal Society for the Prevention of Cruelty to Animals commended Mr Peter Humphrey of Middlesex (U.K.) for his action in saving his goldfish from drowning. Mr Humphrey found the goldfish gasping for air at the surface of his garden pond. He fished it out and discovered that its mouth was jammed open by a pebble. After gently easing the pebble out, he dropped the fish back into the water, where it quickly recovered.

Said an R.S.P.C.A. inspector, "There are not many people who know that a fish could drown if it swallows too much water. I would hate to think how many goldfish owners would have stood by and let the fish drown because they did not know what was wrong."

"The way the fish was behaving," said Mr Humphrey, "it was obvious to me it was drowning. It kept gasping for air on the surface and then sinking." *(109)*

February, 1969

Janice Archer, aged 7, of Harlow, Essex (U.K.), was sitting quietly at her home, picking a winkle with a pin, when it suddenly exploded and set her dress alight. Marine biologists at Plymouth were asked for an opinion on the incident but they did not have the slightest idea how it could have happened. *(110)*

1969

Fred Fletcher, who ran a fishing lodge for many years at Taupo, New Zealand, had an almost inexhaustible fund of stories about the characters he had met at the lodge. Some of the stories were told in a book called *Mr Hundred Per Cent*, by Keith Draper, and this is one of them.

One day I wandered over to the river and saw two anglers fishing the straight -- the water below the bridge parallel with the road and the lake shore. They were about 200 yards apart.

The nearer one was Bill Branson, who had built a house in Taupo town and who lived there until his death a few years back.

"Any luck, Branson?" I called out.

"No," he grunted. "Old Robbie has jumped my possie." He jerked his thumb in the direction of the other angler. It was Colonel Robinson, one of the old members of the Waitahanui school. I wandered down towards him.

"Any fish, Colonel?"

"No," he snapped. "Branson's in my place." *(111)*

January, 1973

Many Japanese love to play a kind of culinary Russian roulette by eating the poisonous puffer fish *(Trepota)*.

Every year hundreds of people die from this deadly delicacy but the only effect has been to swell the numbers of people who are prepared to take the risk.

The puffer, or fugu, has what could almost be described as a cult following. It has even moved poets to verse, for example:

> Last night he and I ate fugu,
> Today I help carry his coffin.

(It probably rhymes in Japanese.)

The species is fairly widely distributed in the Pacific. In Hawaii it is known as *oopuhue* or *keke* and the Hawaiians also consider it a rare delicacy. They adopt the same fatalistic attitude as the Japanese towards the risk.

When removed from the water the puffer swells itself up like a balloon. It maintains this size and shape as long as it is kept out of the water, but if it is returned to its native element it will shrink down to normal size and swim away.

It is the ovaries and liver of the puffer which contain the poison. Called tetrodotoxin, it attacks the nerves and muscles and can kill within minutes. It is so powerful that one ounce of it would be sufficient to kill 56,000 diners.

A licensed fugu chef is one who, apart from experience, has spent two months studying and training and then passed a government examination. The chefs claim that many of the fatalities are due to amateurs who prepare their own meals but fail to slice away the deadly parts in their entirety.

The puffer is usually eaten raw, cut into paper-thin wafers, arranged artistically on the plate or, sometimes, stewed with vegetables.

In rural areas there is a belief that a person suffering from the puffer's poison should be buried neck-deep in a hole. However, this seldom works. The victim almost always finishes up in a deeper, more permanent hole. *(112-113)*

August, 1975

It must have been some sort of a record. Mrs Barbara Wilkinson, of Humberside (U.K.), landed 304 fish in 3 hours during the Ladies' Angling Championships at Hedon, near Hull. *(114)*

November, 1976

At Kosava, on the Danube, fishermen caught a 572-pound sturgeon, estimated to be between 80 and 100 years old, which yielded 97 pounds of caviar. *(115)*

July, 1983

Thirteen stitches in a girl swimmer's foot proved that a local legend at Hurley, Wisconsin, was true. There was a monster fish in Island Lake, a favourite local swimming hole.

For years there had been stories about a 7-foot muskie who had been too smart for the local fishermen. Then, Amber Fairley, aged 13, was swimming in the lake when she felt a set of big, sharp teeth sink into her foot. Judging by the size of the teeth marks, it was a big fish. *(116)*

June, 1984

Andrew Theunissen, a Zimbabwe policeman, knew that Lake Kariba was infested with crocodiles but he had a theory that, because fish were so plentiful in the lake, the crocodiles would not bother to attack people. He was wrong.

One day, he had a headache, and it was hot, so he dived into the lake to cool off. His dive took him head-first into the open jaws of a crocodile.

"It was absolutely terrifying," he said. "It was pitch dark inside the crocodile's mouth. I couldn't see at all. Its top jaw was over the back of my head and his bottom jaw was over my face. There was a terrible noise as the great beast ground its teeth on my skull. It was a very violent, crunching, grinding noise. His teeth were so sharp that they went straight through the flesh of my head and ground on my skull as he tried to crush it."

Theunissen is a strong man and knowing that he was fighting for his life no doubt gave him additional strength. He believes that for a short time he had superhuman strength. At any rate, he was able to force the crocodile's jaws apart and pull his head clear.

"It's amazing how a human being reacts in a situation like that," said Theunissen, "because after the first shock I was no longer afraid. I knew that I was only a couple of metres away from the bank so quickly I released his jaws and kicked away from him with all my might."

Theunissen made it to the bank and staggered out of the water, bleeding profusely from the head, chest and hands. He recovered after hospital treatment. *(117)*

August, 1985

Fishing in a Paris canal, M. Christian Arnt caught a 6-inch fish with extremely sharp teeth. He was curious about what type of fish it was but almost lost a finger while examining it. The fish turned out to be a piranha. *(118)*

August, 1986

The day before the Louisiana Bass Casters Tournament, a fisherman saw a line hanging from a cyprus limb and dangling into the water. He investigated and found, underneath, at the end of the line, a bucket containing five bass, waiting for someone to pull them up from the water on tournament day.

Officials were notified and they broke the second dorsal fin on each fish and returned them to the river-bed in the bucket.

Next day, when Alva Anding produced his catch, including the five fish with broken fins, nothing was said until he accepted the "heavy string" division prize for the day's largest catch. Then he was arrested.

The prize won by Anding was a boat and rig worth $4,500 plus $100 for a win in another category. He pleaded guilty to charges of theft and attempted theft and was sentenced to two years' hard labour. *(119)*

January, 1988

A female pike will lay hundreds of thousands of eggs, but the ultimate survival rate is very, very small, particularly if the young are forced to live in a confined space. Even though there is little difference between them in size, at least initially, brother and sister will eat each other whole until there is only one fish left.

This tiny survival rate is common throughout the whole fish kingdom. An average-sized female cod will lay more than six million eggs at each breeding session but usually only one or two of them will survive to adulthood.

Most fish eggs, or young fish, are eaten by other creatures of one kind or another. Sea fish lay their eggs in plankton where they are eaten in vast quantities by whales.

To compensate for the tremendously high casualty rate, most fish lay huge numbers of eggs. One ling fish was found to have 28 million eggs in her ovaries. *(120)*

August, 1988

There have been many instances where humans in trouble have been helped by dolphins but it must be very rare for a human to be aided by a shark. This happened at Laoag, in the Philippines. A 6-year-old boy was drowning when a giant mako shark pushed him to the shore.

"I saw it happen with my own eyes and I still don't believe it," said a witness, Philip Mortel. "Mako sharks don't help humans, they eat them. But this monster lifted the boy up on its snout and nudged him to safety. It was as gentle as a mother with a new-born baby."

The boy's father, Domingo de Belen, was on the beach when he saw his son carried out to sea by an undertow. Unable to swim, he called out to people, asking them the save the boy. "There were nine or ten people on the beach and I shouted for help. But everything was happening so fast. By the time I got their attention, Mus, my boy, had gone under."

"Then," said another witness, Manuel Redublo, "everyone on the beach watched in stunned silence as the shark swam towards the shore, pushing the boy before it as it came." When it had pushed the child into shallow water, the shark hesitated for a moment, then swung round and disappeared.

The boy, Mus de Belen, was kept in hospital overnight but by the following day he had completely recovered.

Mr Dioscorio Otazu, an expert on marine life, gave what seems to be the most reasonable explanation for the shark's strange behaviour: "From time to time we hear similar reports of sharks overcoming their predatory instincts," he said. "My guess is that they are females with unusually strong maternal instincts. They sense danger and fear in the drowning person and respond as they might for one of their own kind." *(121)*

August, 1988

Most New Yorkers would probably be surprised, if not amazed, to know that giant turtles, with jaws powerful enough to snap a man's hand off, are roaming the sewers, deep beneath their city.

How did they get there? ASPCA spokesman Jeffrey Hon shed some light on the question:

"They get into the sewers during the heavy rains of springtime. The Hudson River gets too much water and gates are opened to allow the water to flow into the East River. There are screens on the gates and they trap the turtles. When they're found, we're called to pick them up."

"They're big!" said Tom Rau, a sewage treatment worker. "I've seen them this big," forming the largest circle he possibly could with his arms. *(122)*

October, 1988

Cleber Salenzi, aged 26, of Santa Maria, Brazil, liked to be the life of the party and one of his favourite stunts was to swallow live goldfish. On one occasion he ordered four dozen goldfish from a pet shop and proceeded to impress his friends by sliding them down his throat. But, this time, although he didn't realise it for a while, something had gone wrong. The pet shop had included a 4-inch piranha in the batch by mistake.

Half-way through his act, Salenzi suddenly doubled over in pain. His friends rushed him to hospital where doctors operated, stitched up the hole in his stomach that had been inflicted by the piranha, and removed the fish.

"He's really very lucky to be alive," said Dr Decio Campos. "The piranha opened a thumb-sized hole in his stomach before gastric acids killed it. If he hadn't come to us when he did, there is no doubt that he would be dead right now. I've never seen anything like it. It was almost as if the piranha had been trying to eat Mr Salenzi from the inside out."

Salenzi declared that the experience would not stop him from swallowing goldfish but he admitted he would make certain what kind of fish he had in his hand in future. *(123)*

November, 1988

A 71-year-old Australian farmer from Proserpine, Queensland, became quite emotional when he was re-united with Charlene, his pet crocodile – even though the croc had snapped off one of his hands with a single bite, almost two years earlier.

"I can't find the words to express how happy I am to have Charlene back home again," said Alf Casey. "We'd been together for 24 years and it truly broke my heart when she was taken from me. I told the game officials over and over again that it wasn't Charlene's fault that I lost my hand. I made a mistake and I paid the price. I asked her one day if she wanted some fish and she looked at me the way she always does when she's hungry. I put my hand in the bucket, but when I pulled it out it was empty. Well, all she knew was that it was feeding time. Unfortunately, when she took a bite, it was my hand that she got. She snapped it right off."

The game officials in Queensland initially intended to shoot the 7-foot crocodile, but when Alf pleaded for its life they decided to send it to a crocodile farm instead. For 23 months Charlene lived at the crocodile farm and throughout that period Alf pleaded for the crocodile to be returned to him. Finally, the game officials relented and allowed the pet croc to return home.

"It was grand getting her back," said Alf. "Like welcoming home a lost love." *(124)*

November, 1988

Two brothers, 8-year-old Chama Bhukoli, and 7-year-old Ulli, of

Musoma, Tanzania, made friends with a giant Nile perch. It took bread from their hands; then it repaid their kindness by eating the 8-year-old.

"It was the most horrifying thing I've ever seen," said Costa Baretto, an eye-witness. "One second the fish was as docile as you please. The next thing I know he had chomped down on one of the boy's arms. Then he pulled him into deep water and disappeared."

Said marine expert, Amin Mushtaque, "These fish are up to 5 feet long and can weigh over 120 pounds. They will eat anything that moves. The Nile perch was first introduced to Lake Victoria in 1968 and it has been nothing but a danger and a problem ever since." *(125)*

February, 1989

Residents in Ipswich, Australia, caught in a violent storm, had to run for cover from a heavy downpour of sardines.

Mrs Debra Degen was walking towards her home when she was suddenly surrounded by scores of bouncing and squirming sardines. "I thought my husband was playing a joke but when I looked around my front lawn they were everywhere; it was frightening."

Ipswich is 30 miles from the coast. *(126)*

March, 1989

On February 26, 1989 a Panamanian fishing vessel took on board a man they found bobbing about in the sea in a white canvas body bag 75 miles south of Bermuda in the Devil's Triangle. He said his name was Michel-Yves Gayan and that he had died of cancer in a Bermuda hospital in 1926 when he was 54 years of age.

The skipper of the fishing boat, Captain Gabriel Diaz, said that Gayan was frightened and disoriented when he was picked up. His first words were, "Where am I?"

154

"When we asked him what he was doing in a body bag," said Captain Diaz, "he told us he was dead. He kept referring to the year 1926. And he told us about his life in France and Bermuda up to that date."

Gayan was taken to Bermuda and handed over to the authorities who took him to a clinic run by Dr Harold Jensen.

Up to this point in the story, we could quite reasonably suspect that it was some strange kind of hoax perpetrated by the man claiming to be Gayan – probably because he was mentally deranged. However, when Dr Jensen made a statement after having investigated the matter, the mystery deepened.

"There is no doubt that the man is who he says he is because we have a death certificate, complete with fingerprints, to prove it," said Dr Jensen. "Don't ask me to explain why or how this man came back to life. I have absolutely no explanation for it. Greater minds than mine are working to solve that mystery right now."

According to documents on file in Bermuda, there certainly was a man named Gayan who moved from France to Bermuda in 1918 and who died from cancer in 1926. He was buried at sea, in accordance with his wishes, wrapped in white canvas.

Dr Jensen said that he had examined pictures taken of Gayan before his death and that he did not appear to have aged.

While being questioned, said Dr Jensen, Gayan spoke in fits and starts and was not always lucid. He seemed to remember being with "glowing white angels" but it was not clear whether he thought he had been in heaven.

Gayan was later transferred to the Zurich Psychiatric Institute where his case was taken over by Dr Charles Greder. "The man has been through something that the human mind can hardly comprehend," said Dr Greder. "He is having great difficulty coping with what happened to him and is not yet able to tell us everything he knows. When he does I am sure that we will hear things that will interest and possibly even benefit all mankind."

155

Dr Greder said it could take many months for him to complete his investigations and that he intended to publish a full scientific report in due course. As far as is known, no further information has been made public regarding the mystery. *(127)*

March, 1989

In December, 1987 Jan Morgan, a woman who runs a pub in Hillswick, a small fishing village in Scotland's rugged Shetland Islands, found a young North Sea seal entangled in a fishing net. The baby seal was almost dead from exhaustion and starvation so Jan freed him from the net and took him to the pub to nurse him back to health.

"I named him Tiny Tim because of the wistful little-boy expression he had," said Jan. "It reminded me of the crippled lad in Dickens's book, *A Christmas Carol.*

"I kept him for about six weeks and he became like a house pet. Even my dog Brian was fond of him. But finally he was well enough to go back to the sea where he belonged. I had tears streaming down my face when I put him into the water."

One year later Tiny Tim returned to pay a visit to his benefactor.

"It's the most thrilling thing that's ever happened to me," said Jan. "The moment I laid eyes on him I knew it was Tiny Tim, the same seal I had cared for the year before. And I could clearly see in his eyes that he recognised me. My first thought was that he had been injured again and had come back to the place where he had gotten help before. But when I examined him, I couldn't find a thing wrong. I can only believe that Tim came back out of love, that he wanted to see me again. When he saw me come out of the house, he started swaying his body and bobbing his head and barking like a hound. I don't know how long he'll stay, but he's free to come and go as he pleases." *(128)*

June, 1989

"Tropical fish are not dumb, as many people think," said Dr

Stoskopf, former chief of medicine at the National Aquarium in Baltimore. "They can be trained. While one in every four American households keeps pet fish, many Americans are unaware of how they will respond to training and affection. They can easily be trained to swim through hoops and beg for food! Some have very distinct personalities with definite likes and dislikes."

Incidentally, one strange ability that fish have is demonstrated by the fact that they will limit their maximum growth to a size which is compatible with the size of the bowl or tank in which they are confined.   *(129-130)*

June, 1989

Five castaways from a shipwreck in the Philippines, dying from lack of food and water, were miraculously saved from certain death when they were towed to safety by a giant turtle. The story was told by one of the men, Jose Cardinas, from his hospital bed in Manila.

"We prayed for a miracle to save us," said Cardinas, "but none of us would have dreamed the miracle would be a turtle." Cardinas said he and his companions abandoned the 150-foot island freighter, *Alberto*, only minutes before it sank in a storm about 100 miles off the southeast tip of Luzon. They had no time to stock their lifeboat with food and water before pushing off.

"We were hit with the full force of the storm," Cardinas said. "Our loading booms were carried away and finally the forward cargo hatch was ripped off and the seas poured into the hold. We threw the rubber lifeboat into the water and managed to scramble aboard just as our ship went down. We drifted for six days without food and not a drop of fresh water to drink. By the third day, we were all very weak from lack of water. We prayed for a miracle or, if not that, a quick death.

"Then on the sixth day, a gigantic turtle swam alongside our boat. It was at least 7 feet long and must have weighed over 1,000 pounds. All we could think of was the food and liquid it could give us if we could kill it. We quickly made a noose from the rope in our survival locker and managed to get it over the turtle's head, but the line slipped over its flippers and got caught on the front of the shell. We tried to free it, but we couldn't get our hands on the turtle because it had swum out in front of the boat.

"Suddenly we noticed that the turtle was towing the boat. On the ninth night, we made out a faint glow on the horizon. We didn't know where we were, but we knew the lights meant there was an island nearby with people on it.

"The next morning, we could see the island, and then we knew it was Luzon. We were home. We were saved and we all gave our thanks to God. By noon, we were inside Manila Bay and we suddenly realised that our boat wasn't moving, we were just drifting in on the tide.

"Before dawn, the turtle had slipped away from the rope and swum away. Obviously it could have escaped at any time, but it took us into safe waters before it left us. The turtle knew we needed help or we would die. Or maybe it somehow knew that to save itself it would have to save us. I don't know, but it towed us home and saved our lives. And we almost ate it!" *(131)*

August, 1989

Jacques Cousteau described in his book *The Whale: Mighty Monarch of the Sea,* an interesting incident in which a mother whale was seen to discipline her calf by whacking it several times with her flippers. The mother swam after her calf and pushed it away from a ship. As Cousteau says, "The blows had every appearance of being slaps and were obviously administered to teach the baby not to confuse a ship's hull with a mother's stomach."

But mother whales also use their flippers to show affection to their young. They use them like hands to fondle their babies.

158

Adult whales demonstrate a caring attitude towards one another. Whilst migrating, they travel at the speed of the slowest baby in the group and if an adult whale is injured or sick the other whales will help it. Sometimes, two healthy whales will cradle the weak one between them; sometimes they will support it on their backs.

Whales apparently like Beethoven's music. The Russians discovered this five years ago when they attempted to rescue 3,000 beluga whales trapped in the Bering Sea. Icebreakers had smashed an escape path for the whales through the ice but the animals were confused and frightened and refused to move.

Attempts were made to calm them by playing music through loudspeakers. The whales did not appear to appreciate military music, or jazz, or rock. It was only when they heard the strains of Beethoven that they were reassured and began to follow the ships through the narrow channel to safety.   *(132)*

September, 1989

A weird story from the Devil's Triangle concerns Barney Spooner, skipper of a fishing boat, who died on board of a heart attack and was buried at sea off Bermuda. Then, 72 hours later, he was fished out of the sea – alive!

With him when he died were his 64 year-old wife, Lillian, their grandsons, Jonathan and Bartholomeu and three crew members.

"There's no doubt in our minds that Grandfather died," 27-year-old Jonathan said. "He just keeled over and that was it. He had no heartbeat, no pulse and no breathing. He was dead. We were going to take him into St. George and notify the authorities, but Grandmother wouldn't hear of it. She said that he had always insisted that he be buried at sea and that's just the way it would be – then and there. So that's what we did. We wrapped him in a blanket, tied it up and attached an old anchor and threw him into the sea he loved."

According to Captain Spooner, he spent the next 72 hours in

some kind of limbo of the lost. "I saw them all," he said, "the sightless eyes, the lifeless shapes, the ghost ships and the phantom planes of that unholy place. It was like some awful nightmare, but I wasn't afraid. They were all dead. But I knew that I was as dead as they were. Yet I had the feeling that I wasn't really one of them ... that I was merely an observer. I had the feeling I was in a world where I didn't belong.

"I saw the lost ships – the *Cyclops*, the *Marine Sulphur Queen*, the *Raifuku Maru* and *Witchcraft*. And I saw the planes – the five Navy Avengers, the Star Tiger and so many other planes. They were everywhere. And I saw the faces of all the people who had vanished over the decades. There were so many. They flashed by me like a slow-motion film. They had no expression on their faces. They were just images frozen in time."

Captain Spooner said he experienced a peculiar rushing sensation. Then he found he was up in the air looking down and seeing his own body bobbing in the water. "I saw my boat slow, then stop dead. Bartholomeu put the dinghy over the side and rowed over to me. Suddenly, I wasn't above looking down anymore. I was in the water with my eyes wide open – and I was looking up into the face of my grandson. He stared at me as though he was seeing a ghost. Then he just pulled me into the dinghy and rowed back to the boat."

"How his spirit got into that other place," said the captain's wife, "only God knows. But he didn't belong there and he couldn't stay. Maybe the only way he could leave was to come back to the living."

(133)

October, 1989

Sammy is a very tough little goldfish. When his owner, Fergal Parkinson, of Sheffield, England, found him floating in his fish-bowl, he placed the little fellow in an envelope and buried him under two inches of soil in the garden.

Later, as he passed Sammy's grave, Fergal noticed something

moving beneath the soil, then Sammy's head appeared, followed by his body. Fergal took the fish inside and put him back in his bowl. Sammy spat out a mouthful of dirt, then began swimming around, as good as new!

"I couldn't believe it when he wriggled out of the ground where I had buried him. I had to look twice before I could believe my eyes. He had been out of the water for at least 40 minutes, and goodness knows how long he had been floating on the surface of his bowl before I discovered him. He is a very tough little fish."

A South Yorkshire veterinarian, Dr Mark Hallam, later examined Sammy and pronounced him quite fit and healthy but the vet could not explain how Sammy was able to survive such an ordeal.

"It is quite exceptional, and there is no obvious explanation," he said. "For fish to survive out of water for as long as this one did does seem to be a remarkable thing."   (134)

November, 1989

The police in Clearwater, Fla., received a tip-off telling them the exact spot where a body had been buried.

They roped off the area, began digging and sifting the earth and were thus busily engaged when a passer-by told them he had seen a man burying a huge fish there a week before. They carried on, just in case, but their digging eventually uncovered the remains of a 500-pound grouper. It wasn't April Fool's Day, but the police realised that they'd been had.   (135)

December, 1989

Piranhas have proved to be useful on one occasion, at least. At Worthing, England, money was being collected for a hospital charity by means of a wishing well. The trouble was that thieves kept raiding the money. Carlos Bellone, the custodian of the well, found a good solution. He put a pair of piranhas in the well. That solved the problem.   (136)

December, 1989

A blunder by the public works department at Uttar Pradesh, India, has resulted in a weird new danger for people who swim in the Ganges River. They risk death from bloodthirsty turtles!

The department released into the river a specially-bred type of soft-shelled river turtle as a pollution measure. The department's scientists believed that the turtles would pick the flesh from the untold thousands of partially-burned corpses that are dumped into the river each year but that they would not attack the living.

The scientists were wrong. Up to December, 1989 three people were known to have been killed by the turtles and many more injured.

"In three separate incidents," said Rajesh Mohan, an official of the public works department, "people have been pulled under the water and devoured by these man-eating beasts. Their bones were picked clean in just a matter of minutes. And these are only the reported deaths. Who knows how many other unfortunates have been eaten that we don't know about."

Ram Jain was on a religious pilgrimage to the Ganges when he and his small son were attacked.

"We were in the water when my son, Suman, aged three, suddenly disappeared beneath the surface. I lunged toward where he'd been standing only a moment before. I felt a sharp stinging sensation on my leg as if I were being bitten, but I ignored it in my concern for my son. Somehow I located him and pulled him to safety before he was eaten alive. As it was, his left foot was mangled so badly, it had to be amputated."

Officials are at a loss to know what to do about the problem. Thousands of people bathe in the holy waters of the river every day. They've been warned of the danger but the warning serves no purpose. "They're still going to bathe there, no matter what the danger, because it's a religious experience for them," said

Rajesh Mohan. *(137)*

The Orca or Killer Whale

Explorers and scientists have returned from the Antarctic with many interesting stories about the aquatic inhabitants of that part of the world. Among the most fascinating are those about the orca, or killer whale. The early explorers, particularly those in Scott's expeditions, expressed often the dread they felt for these awful creatures.

The killer whale is a member of the cetacean family which also includes dolphins, porpoises and whales. However, the killer whale is the only member of the family that will attack its kin. One 24-foot specimen, which was captured, was found to have in its stomach the remains of 13 porpoises and 14 seals. *(138)*

The orca grows up to 30 feet in length and when it speeds in to attack its prey it may easily be identified by its high, triangular-shaped dorsal fin.

Killers will attack even the largest of whales but when they are after this kind of prey they hunt in a pack. They first tear at the lips and tongue and when the victim has died from loss of blood the rest of the carcase is consumed.

Scott's men told of seeing the killers hunt seals that were on ice floes. A killer would raise itself up out of the water and lean its head on the edge of the ice floe. The resulting tilt would cause the seal to slide helplessly across the ice towards the jaws of the hunter. *(139)*

Scott's photographer, Herbert Ponting, had a narrow escape from the killers. He had noticed a pack of them converging on an ice floe on which two of the expedition's dogs were tied up and he moved to the edge of the ice and began photographing the drama. Suddenly, he realised that he, also, had been targeted. The killers began thumping their bodies into the ice beneath his feet, breaking it into fragments. *(140)*

On another occasion, three men and three ponies were trapped on an ice floe when a large piece of ice broke off unexpectedly and began drifting towards the open sea. They found themselves "in the middle of a floating pack of broken-up ice".

Using a 12-foot sledge as a bridge, men and ponies crossed from one piece of ice to the next, in an effort to regain the solid ice Barrier. And, all the time, hundreds of killer whales cruised around, gazing at men and animals in their predicament and waiting for their opportunity.

"The killers were too interested in us to be pleasant," said Bowers, leader of the party. "They had a habit of bobbing up and down perpendicularly, so as to see over the edge of a floe ... The huge black and yellow heads with sickening pigs' eyes only a few yards from us at times, and always around us, are among the most disconcerting recollections I have of that day. The immense fins were bad enough, but when they started the perpendicular dodge they were positively beastly."

Eventually, the three men escaped with one pony, but the killer whales got the other two.   (141)

Penguins

Everyone who visits the Antarctic seems to develop a soft spot for penguins and many amusing stories have been told about them. One story concerns their odd behaviour when they wish to return to the water. Observers have commented that it looks like a game, but actually it is a very serious business – a matter of life and death, in fact, for the penguins.

Penguins have a deadly enemy in the sea leopard and their problem when they want to return to the sea is that one of these fierce animals may be lurking beneath the surface of the water. The penguins solve the problem in their own peculiar way. First, large numbers of them will cluster together on the ice, close to the water's edge. Then, somehow, they select an unfortunate guinea pig – probably the male who is at the bottom of the pecking order at that particular time – who is shouldered to the edge of the ice and pushed in.

The remainder, from their safe position on the shore, peer anxiously at the water. If he comes up, they all dive in to join him.

Helicopters have been put to considerable use by scientific expeditions to the Antarctic during recent years and it soon became apparent that penguins were absolutely fascinated by these aircraft. They just could not take their eyes off the choppers. The shores of a bay would be packed with penguins, probably a million or more, and every pair of eyes would be on the helicopter.

This led the helicopter pilots to play a little joke on the penguins. Firstly, they would fly across the bay, out over the water, then return in the opposite direction. The heads of the penguins would slowly turn from left to right, then from right to left, just like humans watching a tennis match played in slow motion.

Then the helicopter would swing around and fly towards the penguins. They would continue to eye it intently, craning their necks upwards until it arrived directly above them. The helicopter would continue on. And a million penguins would flip over onto the ice on their backs.

9. The Fish Story To End All Fish Stories

I will lead up to "the fish story to end all fish stories" gradually. First, a couple of somewhat similar occurrences which are more easily believable.

In February, 1923, at Glenmore Lake, Orange County, New York, thousands of fish were smothered by a cover of thick ice from shore to shore. The ice was more than two feet thick and on top of this was a foot or more of snow.

The township of Florida obtained its water supply from the lake and when their drinking water became objectionable, they complained to the State Conservation Commission. When a hole was cut through the ice, thousands of dead fish came to the surface and were washed over the dam. More holes were cut. As the dead fish were washed away, thousands of live fish, in search of air, appeared at the holes.   *(1)*

A lagoon at Stony Brook, Long Island, became a hive of activity in January, 1939, when word spread through the community that thousands of fish were available for the taking.   At least 400 people accepted the invitation and set out to collect the windfall by whatever means they were able to employ, from automobiles and trucks, down to wheelbarrows and paper bags.

The lagoon was situated on the property of the Oldfield Country Club, which had closed for the winter.

Two men had gone there to dig for clams. They decided to dig a hole through the ice and found the lagoon was packed full of fish – big sea bass which had apparently been trapped there when the tide went out.

The two clammers quickly got about 1,000 pounds of fish out, probably hoping that they could keep their find a secret, but word soon spread and they were joined by hundreds of other people.

The general opinion was that the fish had probably swum into the harbour to feed. They weighed from about 3 pounds up, the biggest being 15 pounds.

A couple of the axe-wielding crowd fell into the icy water but they were promptly pulled out by their friends and suffered no serious harm. *(2)*

The event that I consider to be "the fish story to end all fish stories" occurred back in 1860 and is known as the Kekoskee fish story. The best known version was that originally told during the 1860's by Dr Clark, of Mayville, Wis.:

These events happened before the war. They are so singular and improbable that I always hesitate about telling the story. You will probably laugh at me and not believe me, yet every word of this is true.

The Winter of 1860 was very cold. At that time a vast lake covered the whole ground where Horicon Marsh now is. This lake was full of fish, and when the ice had frozen deep over every portion of the lake these fish became distressed for air. The Rock River, as you know, is a lively stream here, and, as you have noticed, it has a stretch of swift water just below the great dam at Kekoskee. This dam existed at the time of the story. You have looked with your own eyes upon the very spot where these startling incidents occurred.

The fish, unable to breathe in the half-solid lake, crowded up the live channel of the Rock River, making for the hole which the swift water kept open in the ice below Kekoskee Dam. Most of these fish were bullheads, and no river of salmon ever equalled this run of bullheads. It is six miles from the lake to the Kekoskee Dam, and the ice on the river was 2 feet thick, yet the whole bed of the river – 40 yards wide – was for six miles so packed with bullheads that the heavy covering of tough ice in places rolled and tossed like the waves of the sea, so desperate was the struggle of the horny host beneath it.

The first arrival of the run of the fish at the open hole was marked by a geyser-like eruption of bullheads, 50 feet across and about 12 feet high. The pressure of the fish behind was simply enormous. The fish could not get back in the water, and so slid out on the ice, covering it in every direction for hundreds of yards to a depth varying from 6 inches to 2 feet.

The air was filled with a strange, low murmuring sound, which could be heard nearly a mile around. Old settlers say they have never heard such a sound since. Dreading some unknown calamity, they hastened to the spot, and there, as you may suppose, their dread was turned to joy.

Before noon of that day every team of the whole neighbourhood was at the dam, hauling bullheads. The amount of bullheads taken from that spot I hesitate to state, for fear you will not believe it. You cannot believe it. I do not ask you to believe it. No one believes it. They always laugh at us when we tell this story, and think we have gone crazy. In Wisconsin the term "Kekoskee man" is used to designate one who has a wheel in his head. No Kekoskee man has been believed on oath or admitted to a jury in Wisconsin since 1860. This unearned reputation has ruined the town. You see it as it is, silent, almost deserted, a few empty buildings standing as monuments to a town martyred unto ruin by too strict an adherence to the truth. For every word of this story is true.

If you will come with me about a mile out in the country, I will introduce you to the widow Sneider, now an old lady. The widow Sneider will tell you that on one morning she counted 900 wagon-loads of bullheads on their way from the geyser below the dam. This was only one morning, and the run lasted for two weeks. Of course, this number of wagons represented only a part of those which passed, and this was on only one road of several leading out into the country.

The bullheads were shovelled into the wagons like potatoes, and the regular price was 25 cents a load, a nominal sum, to cover the shovelling only. One man who shovelled there bought a farm in this vicinity with the money so earned.

The bullheads were hauled out into the country and used largely for manure. There is no richer land in Wisconsin than this has been since 1860. All the farmers fed the bullheads to their hogs, and for two years after that you couldn't get a decent piece of pork in this part of the State. It was all fishy. The hogs all took naturally to worms and liver after that, and some of them evinced rudimentary gills behind the ears. Oh, I don't blame you for doubting this. They all do.

There was a ford on the road at this point of the river, but the wagons could not get into the water. After the first eruption of bullheads had subsided planks were laid across on the living pontoon bridge of fish, and on these the teams crossed.

Even after the run had subsided very much, dogs and children were known to run across the open hole on the backs of the bullheads. Still later in the run, after the fish had thinned out a great deal, a man well known in this community – Julius Cornell – slipped from the ice and fell into the hole. He could not get into the water for the fish. You smile at this. I do not blame you. We are used to it. No one ever believes this story.

After the bullheads thinned out so you could get a spear through them as they lay in a matted layer, it was discovered that there were layers of bass and pickerel.

Of course everybody that Winter lived on bullheads and they were used in many ways. As I have said, the farmers fed them to their hogs. We had a lazy sort of expressman here named Brush, and he owned a fallen-down old horse which dated back to the Mexican war and was called Santa Anna. Brush insisted that he was too poor to buy Santa Anna hay, so he fed him bullheads all Winter, and that was everything the horse had to eat for four months. Oh, laugh, if you want to, we're used to it. But I'll take you out and show you Santa Anna, a good healthy sort of a horse today. Brush has moved to Bayfield, but you ask any citizen of this town if Santa Anna didn't live on bullheads, and if he don't tell you just what I have I'll retract the whole story.

You needn't think for a minute that I'm talking to you out of my head. These things are all facts and you can get all the proof you want. You just go out alone; don't take me along, but just stop any citizen of Mayville you meet and ask him how about the Kekoskee bullheads. That's all I ask you to do. You just sift this story and see if you don't find it true.

The New York Times reprinted this story on October 16, 1892. And, accompanying it, were comments by a reporter who had earlier been sent to Mayville to determine the truth of the matter. He went a skeptic, but he returned a believer:

We did sift the story and we did find it true. That is the singular thing about the story, and that is why I call it the most remarkable story I ever heard. The facts themselves are not beyond the range of imagination, but to have a whole community rise up and testify to their truth – that proves that imagination has nothing to do with it, and that the facts are facts pure and simple. Ordinarily one man tells a fish story. Here 200 tell it and tell it just the same. The evidence is legal, convincing, overwhelming. In the total it makes up the grandest fish story there ever was. I tell it here, but it is nothing. No one man can tell it. It takes a whole town to tell it. To hear it aright you must go to Mayville. There the whole town will tell you this story. You dare not, you cannot, doubt it. You will believe, and you will feel, as we did there, that the entire chain of circumstances in this case constitutes the most remarkable incident in the history of a lifetime.

The reporter interviewed everyone he could find who had lived in the district in 1860 and he found that, no matter whom he talked to, the details of the story never varied. He decided that there was no question that the story was true.

Despite his certainty in this regard, our reporter was obviously more than a little concerned that *he* might be branded a liar by doubting Thomases and he concluded his comments with the following:

I should dislike to have this story meet the ridicule with which I treated it before I had become convinced of its entire truthfulness, and any doubting allusions to it I shall treat as personal aspersions. If the proof offered here is not sufficient there is plenty more in Mayville. *(3)*

In the hope of a future expanded edition, or, better still, additional volumes, I would be pleased to hear from readers who have interesting fish stories to report, or unusual photographs which relate to fishing. Please write to me at the following address:

P. O. Box 3068,
Weston Creek,
Canberra,
A.C.T. 2611,
Australia.

Ken Byron
1994

References

1. **My Favourite Fish Stories**
   1. *The Times*, 27 Nov. 1839
   2. *The Times*, 15 Aug. 1919
   3. *The New York Times*, 22 Dec. 1892
   4. *The New York Times*, 17 Feb. 1929
   5. *The New York Times*, 10 May 1936
   6. *The New York Times*, 27 Dec. 1938
   7. *The Sydney Morning Herald*, 17 Jun. 1956

2. **Some Big Ones That Got Away**
   1. *The Times*, 23 Oct. 1848
   2. *The New York Times*, 27 Apr. 1883
   3. *The New York Times*, 12 Mar. 1921
   4. *The New York Times*, 19 Jun. 1935
   5. *The New York Times*, 23 Aug. 1937
   6. *The New York Times*, 26 May 1938
   7. *The Argus*, 12 Jan. 1940
   8. *The New York Times*, 21 Apr. 1941
   9. *The Sydney Morning Herald*, 8 Oct. 1950
   10. *The Sydney Morning Herald*, 21 Apr. 1955
   11. *The Sydney Morning Herald*, 12 Apr. 1959
   12. *The Times*, 23 Jan. 1968
   13. *The Times*, 19 Aug. 1968
   14. *National Enquirer*, 12 Dec. 1989

3. **And Some That Didn't Get Away**
   1. *The New York Times*, 20 Aug. 1860, reprinted 5 Jul. 1908
   2. *The New York Times*, 11 Aug. 1907
   3. *The New York Times*, 7 Jul. 1922
   4. *The New York Times*, 6 Jun. 1925
   5. *The Sydney Morning Herald*, 20 Jul. 1927
   6. *The New York Times*, 21 Feb. 1931
   7. *The New York Times*, 25 Jul. 1935
   8. *The Times*, 20 Sep. 1937
   9. *The Sydney Morning Herald*, 30 Dec. 1949
   10. *The New York Times*, 23 Apr. 1950
   11. *The Times*, 25 Nov. 1952
   12. *The Times*, 28 May 1958
   13. *The Times*, 30 May 1958

14. *The Times*, 17 Sep. 1959
15. *The Times*, 7 Jun. 1963
16. *The Sydney Morning Herald*, 8 Apr. 1954
17. *The Sun-Herald,* Australia, 1 Nov. 1959
18. *The Sydney Morning Herald*, 16 Nov. 1960
19. *The Times*, 15 May 1967
20. *The Times*, 11 Jun. 1977
21. *The Washington Post*, 21 Jan. 1979
22. *Wot a Whopper*, Bob Staines, Lansdowne Press, Sydney, 1982
23. *The New York Times*, 8 Aug. 1986

4. Queer Fish

1. *The Times*, 18 Aug. 1801
2. *The Times*, 4 Nov. 1850
3. *The Times*, 6 Nov. 1867
4. *The New York Times*, 29 July 1877
5. *The New York Times*, 27 Apr. 1883
6. *The Times*, 7 Aug. 1906
7. *The Times*, 15 Aug. 1906
8. *The Times*, 9 Aug. 1906
9. *The Times*, 17 Aug. 1906
10. *The Argus*, 26 May 1913
11. *The New York Times*, 26 Sep. 1922
12. *The New York Times*, 31 July 1925
13. *The New York Times*, 13 Jan. 1926
14. *The New York Times*, 9 Oct. 1927
15. *The Sydney Morning Herald*, 3 Oct. 1927
16. *The New York Times*, 5 May 1929
17. *The New York Times*, 13 Sep. 1929
18. *The New York Times*, 2 Feb. 1930
19. *The New York Times*, 18 Jan. 1932
20. *The New York Times*, 5 Jun. 1933
21. *The New York Times*, 10 Aug. 1934
22. *The Argus*, 14 Aug. 1934
23. *The Argus*, 23 Nov. 1934
24. *The Argus*, 26 Nov. 1934
25. *The New York Times*, 9 Dec. 1934
26. *The New York Times*, 23 Mar. 1935
27. *The Argus*, 31 Jul. 1935
28. *The New York Times*, 7 Jan. 1940
29. *The Argus*, 3 Jan. 1948

30. *The Sydney Morning Herald*, 3 Feb. 1949
31. *The Sydney Morning Herald*, 11 Feb. 1949
32. *The Sydney Morning Herald*, 9 Sep. 1949
33. *The Sydney Morning Herald*, 16 Nov. 1953
34. *The Sydney Morning Herald*, 5 Nov. 1960
35. *The Times*, 7 July 1970
36. *Wot a Whopper*, Bob Staines, Lansdowne Press, Sydney, 1982
37. *The Times*, 14 Sep. 1983
38. *Truth*, Australia, 13 Aug. 1983
39. *The New York Times*, 6 Oct. 1929
40. *The New York Times*, 27 Aug. 1935
41. *The Sydney Morning Herald*, 27 Mar. 1960
42. *Strange Stories: Amazing Facts, Reader's Digest*, Sydney, 1975
43. *Supernature*, Lyall Watson, Coronet Books, London, 1974
44. *Under the Great Barrier Reef*, Richard Lurie, Jarrolds Publishers, London, 1966
45. *Reader's Digest Book of Facts*, Sydney, 1985
46. *The New York Times*, 30 Dec. 1952
47. *Reader's Digest Book of Facts*, Sydney, 1985
48. *The Sun-Herald*, Australia, 8 Oct. 1989
49. *National Enquirer*, 29 Mar. 1988
50. *National Enquirer*, 18 Oct. 1988

5. That's A Funny Way To Fish!

1. *The Times*, 13 Jan. 1786
2. *The Times*, 29 Nov. 1787
3. *The Times*, 28 Aug. 1790
4. *The Times*, 8 Jan. 1818
5. *The Times*, 12 Jan. 1824
6. *The Times*, 23 Oct. 1829
7. *The Times*, 15 Dec. 1841
8. *The Times*, 12 Mar. 1845
9. *The Times*, 3 Jun. 1848
10. *The Times*, 18 Jul. 1853
11. *The New York Times*, 25 Jul. 1897
12. *The New York Times*, 13 Jul. 1924
13. *The New York Times*, 12 Sep. 1926
14. *The New York Times*, 23 Oct. 1928
15. *The New York Times*, 20 Sep. 1931
16. *The Sydney Morning Herald*, 7 Jan. 1932
17. *The New York Times*, 2 Jan. 1933

18. *The Sydney Morning Herald*, 12 Jan. 1933
19. *The Sydney Morning Herald*, 1 Feb. 1933
20. *The New York Times*, 21 Jun. 1935
21. *The New York Times*, 25 July 1935
22. *The New York Times*, 7 Oct. 1935
23. *The New York Times*, 22 Dec. 1935
24. *The New York Times*, 10 Nov. 1935
25. *The New York Times*, 3 Aug. 1936
26. *The New York Times*, 22 Sep. 1936
27. *The Argus*, 23 Apr. 1937
28. *The New York Times*, 2 May 1937
29. *The New York Times*, 17 May 1937
30. *The New York Times*, 8 Jun. 1937
31. *The New York Times*, 19 Jun. 1937
32. *The New York Times*, 23 Jun. 1937
33. *The New York Times*, 22 Jul. 1937
34. *The New York Times*, 10 Jul. 1937
35. *The New York Times*, 18 Jul. 1937
36. *The Argus*, 19 Aug. 1937
37. *The New York Times*, 18 Jan. 1938
38. *The New York Times*, 3 Apr. 1938
39. *The New York Times*, 30 May 1938
40. *The New York Times*, 21 May 1939
41. *The New York Times*, 7 Jul. 1941
42. *The New York Times*, 21 Aug. 1941
43. *The New York Times*, 26 Mar. 1942
44. *The New York Times*, 20 Jul. 1943
45. *The Sydney Morning Herald*, 14 Jul. 1945
46. *The Times*, 18 Feb. 1946
47. *The Argus*, 22 Jun. 1946
48. *The Argus*, 10 Mar. 1947
49. *The Argus*, 18 Oct. 1947
50. *The New York Times*, 11 Apr. 1948
51. *The Argus*, 4 Sep. 1948
52. *The Sydney Morning Herald*, 5 Mar. 1950
53. *The New York Times*, 23 Apr. 1950
54. Ibid
55. *The Sydney Morning Herald*, 4 Apr. 1951
56. *The Sydney Morning Herald*, 26 Nov. 1951
57. *The Sydney Morning Herald*, 17 Feb. 1952

58. *The Sydney Morning Herald*, 28 Jun. 1953
59. *The Sydney Morning Herald*, 15 Jul. 1953
60. *The Sydney Morning Herald*, 25 Jan. 1957
61. *The New York Times*, 16 Feb. 1937
62. *The New York Times*, 24 Apr. 1939
63. *The Sydney Morning Herald*, 26 May 1957
64. *The Sydney Morning Herald*, 14 Jul. 1957
65. *The Times*, 5 Aug. 1958
66. *The Times*, 27 Aug. 1959
67. *The Times*, 29 Nov. 1962
68. *The New York Times*, 2 Apr. 1936
69. *The New York Times*, 11 Jun. 1936
70. *The Times*, 12 Feb. 1962
71. *The Sydney Morning Herald*, 1 Sep. 1958
72. *The Times*, 9 Jun. 1967
73. *Mr Hundred Per Cent,* Keith Draper, A.H. & A.W. Reed, Sydney, 1969
74. *Wot a Whopper*, Bob Staines, Lansdowne Press, Sydney, 1982
75. Ibid
76. Ibid
77. Ibid
78. Ibid
79. *Reflections from the Water's Edge*, John Bailey, Crowood Press, London, 1987

6.   And When I Cut It Open ...

1. *The Times*, 6 Dec. 1787
2. *The Times*, 7 Aug. 1829
3. *The Times*, 27 Apr. 1837
4. *The Times*, 10 Dec. 1840
5. *The Times*, 4 Jul. 1844
6. *The Times*, 20 Sep. 1855
7. *The New York Times*, 4 May 1928
8. *The Sydney Morning Herald*, 30 Nov. 1934
9. *The New York Times*, 22 Dec. 1939
10. *The Times*, 9 Feb. 1967
11. *Wot a Whopper*, Bob Staines, Lansdowne Press, Sydney, 1982
12. *The Times*, 13 Sep. 1848
13. *The Times*, 25 May 1865
14. *The Times*, 2 Aug. 1872
15. *The Sydney Morning Herald*, 18 Dec. 1930
16. *The New York Times*, 22 Apr. 1932

17. *The New York Times*, 22 Feb. 1938
18. *The New York Times*, 17 Apr. 1938
19. *The New York Times*, 7 Aug. 1938
20. *The Argus*, 11 Apr. 1939
21. *The New York Times*, 5 Sep. 1945
22. *The Argus*, 4 Jun. 1949
23. *The Sydney Morning Herald*, 22 Jun. 1949
24. *The Times*, 29 Dec. 1952
25. *The Sydney Morning Herald*, 30 Dec. 1956
26. *Wot a Whopper*, Bob Staines, Lansdowne Press, Sydney, 1982
27. *Weekly World News*, 29 Nov. 1988
28. *Weekly World News*, 24 Jan. 1989
29. *Weekly World News*, 17 Oct. 1989

7.   Dolphin Stories
1. *Home Is the Sea: For Whales*, Sarah R. Riedman and Elton T. Gustafson, The World's Work (1913) Ltd, U.K., 1968
2. *Dolphin, Dolphin*, Wade Doak, Hodder & Stoughton, New Zealand, 1981
3. *Home Is the Sea: For Whales*
4. Ibid
5. *Dolphin, Dolphin*
6. *Home Is the Sea: For Whales*
7. *Dolphin, Dolphin*
8. *Psychic Pets*, Barbara Woodhouse, New English Library, U.K., 1981
9. *Dolphin, Dolphin*
10. *Home is the Sea: For Whales*
11. *Dolphins*, Antony Alpers, John Murray Ltd, London, 1963
12. *National Enquirer*, 19 Apr. 1988
13. *Dolphin, Dolphin*
14. *Psychic Pets*
15. *Weekly World News*, 22 Nov. 1988

8.   You Wouldn't Believe It!
1. *The Times*, 13 Oct. 1787
2. *The Times*, 26 Aug. 1808
3. *The Times*, 8 Dec. 1824
4. *The Times*, 28 Aug. 1839
5. *The Times*, 29 Aug. 1843
6. *The Times*, 1 Jan. 1847
7. *The Times*, 27 Nov. 1847
8. *The Times*, 8 Nov. 1854
9. *The Times*, 5 Nov. 1856

10. *The Times*, 22 Sep. 1858
11. *The Times*, 22 Sep. 1862
12. *The Times*, 3 Nov. 1864
13. *The Times*, 29 Aug. 1874
14. *The Times*, 7 Dec. 1874
15. *The New York Times*, 2 May 1875
16. Ibid
17. *The Times*, 20 Apr. 1880
18. *The Argus*, 5 Apr. 1947
19. *The New York Times*, 7 June 1911
20. *The Times*, 13 Dec. 1921
21. *The Times*, 19 Dec. 1921
22. *The Argus*, 3 May 1922
23. *The New York Times,* 20 Feb. 1926
24. *The New York Times*, 30 Jan. 1927
25. *The New York Times*, 26 Aug. 1927
26. *The New York Times*, 5 Sep. 1928
27. *The New York Times*, 31 Oct. 1928
28. *The Argus*, 4 Feb. 1929
29. *The New York Times*, 3 Aug. 1930
30. *The Sydney Morning Herald*, 10 Nov. 1930
31. *The New York Times,* 20 Mar. 1932
32. *The New York Times*, 25 Apr. 1932
33. *The Argus*, 5 Apr. 1932
34. *The Sydney Morning Herald*, 31 Dec. 1932
35. *The Sydney Morning Herald*, 9 May 1933
36. *The New York Times*, 28 Oct. 1933
37. *The Sydney Morning Herald*, 15 Dec. 1934
38. *The New York Times*, 7 Apr. 1935
39. *The New York Times*, 14 Apr. 1935
40. *The Sydney Morning Herald*, 4 May 1935
41. *The New York Times*, 30 Jun. 1935
42. *The Times*, 3 Aug. 1935
43. *The New York Times*, 23 Oct. 1935
44. *The New York Times*, 3 Aug. 1937
45. *The Sydney Morning Herald*, 31 Aug. 1937
46. *The Argus*, 13 Dec. 1937
47. *The New York Times*, 30 Apr. 1938
48. *The New York Times*, 29 Apr. 1938
49. *The New York Times*, 22 May 1938

50. *The New York Times*, 12 Jun. 1938
51. *The New York Times*, 29 May 1938
52. *The Argus*, 21 Jul. 1938
53. *The New York Times*, 4 Aug. 1938
54. *The New York Times*, 20 Apr. 1939
55. *The New York Times*, 19 Jul. 1939
56. *The New York Times*, 12 Aug. 1939
57. *The New York Times*, 19 Aug. 1939
58. *The New York Times*, 18 Sep. 1939
59. *The Canberra Times*, 2 Apr. 1985
60. *The New York Times*, 25 July 1935
61. *The New York Times*, 19 Sep. 1939
62. *The New York Times*, 7 Oct. 1939
63. *The Argus*, 16 Dec. 1940
64. *The New York Times*, 21 June 1941
65. *The New York Times*, 7 Sep. 1941
66. *The New York Times*, 24 Oct. 1941
67. *The Argus*, 17 Nov. 1945
68. *The New York Times*, 12 Aug. 1947
69. *Stranger Than Science*, Frank Edwards, Pan Books, London 1963
70. *Home Is the Sea: For Whales*, S.R. Riedman & E.T. Gustafson, The World's Work (1913) Ltd. U.K., 1968
71. Ibid
72. *The Argus*, 20 Mar. 1948
73. *The Argus*, 14 Sep. 1948
74. *The Argus*, 4 Sep. 1948
75. *The Argus,* 16 Oct. 1948
76. *The New York Times*, 16 Nov. 1948
77. *The Argus*, 4 Dec. 1948
78. *The New York Times*, 3 Feb. 1949
79. *The Sydney Morning Herald*, 25 Sep. 1949
80. *The Sydney Morning Herald*, 25 Feb. 1950
81. *The New York Times,* 23 Apr. 1950
82. Ibid.
83. Ibid.
84. Ibid.
85. *The Sydney Morning Herald*, 2 Apr. 1950
86. *The Sydney Morning Herald*, 25 Apr. 1952
87. *The Sydney Morning Herald*, 22 Jul. 1952
88. *The Sydney Morning Herald*, 13 Oct. 1953

89. *The Sydney Morning Herald*, 14 Apr. 1954
90. *The Sydney Morning Herald*, 30 Jun. 1954
91. *The Sydney Morning Herald*, 26 Jul. 1954
92. *The Sydney Morning Herald*, 18 Feb. 1955
93. *The Sydney Morning Herald*, 9 Apr. 1955
94. *The Sydney Morning Herald*, 24 Feb. 1956
95. *The Sydney Morning Herald*, 21 Apr. 1956
96. *The Sydney Morning Herald*, 23 Apr. 1957
97. *The Sydney Morning Herald*, 7 May 1957
98. *The Sydney Morning Herald,* 30 Dec. 1958
99. *The Sydney Morning Herald*, 3 Aug. 1959
100. *The Sydney Morning Herald*, 13 Sep. 1959
101. *The Sydney Morning Herald*, 6 Apr. 1961
102. *The Times*, 4 Feb. 1966
103. *The Canberra Times*, 17 May 1983
104. *The Times*, 10 Dec. 1962
105. *Under the Great Barrier Reef*, Richard Lurie, Jarrolds Publishers, London, 1966
106. Ibid.
107. *The Times*, 29 Mar. 1967
108. *The Times,*7 Apr. 1967
109. *The Times*, 13 Aug. 1968
110. *The Times*, 28 Feb. 1969
111. *Mr Hundred Per Cent*, Keith Draper, A.H. & A.W. Reed, Sydney, 1969
112. *The Washington Post*, 28 Jan. 1973
113. *The New York Times,* 6 Oct. 1929
114. *The Times*, 19 Aug. 1975
115. *The Times*, 17 Nov. 1976
116. *The Canberra Times*, 19 Jul. 1983
117. *Star Enquirer*, Australia, 20 Jun. 1984
118. *The Times*, 7 Aug. 1985
119. *The New York Times*, 4 Aug. 1986
120. *National Enquirer*, 26 Jan. 1988
121. *Weekly World News*, 16 Aug. 1988
122. Ibid.
123. *Weekly World News*, 18 Oct. 1988
124. *Weekly World News,* 1 Nov. 1988
125. *Weekly World News*, 29 Nov. 1988
126. *Daily Mirror*, Australia, 7 Feb. 1989
127. *Weekly World News*, 28 Mar. 1989

128. *Weekly World News*, 7 Mar. 1989
129. *Weekly World News*, 6 Jun. 1989
130. *The Argus*, 5 Jun. 1948
131. *Weekly World News,* 27 Jun. 1989
132. *Reader's Digest*, Aug. 1989
133. *Weekly World News,* 26 Sep. 1989
134. *Weekly World News,* 3 Oct. 1989
135. *Weekly World News*, 14 Nov. 1989
136. *Weekly World News*, 19 Dec. 1989
137. Ibid
138. *Home Is the Sea: For Whales,* S.R. Riedman & E.T. Gustafson, The World's Work (1913) Ltd, U.K., 1968
139. *Dolphins*, Antony Alpers, John Murray Ltd, London, 1963
140. Ibid
141. *Antarctica,* Frank Debenham, Herbert Jenkins Ltd, London, 1959

9. The Fish Story To End All Fish Stories

1. *The New York Times*, 28 Feb. 1923
2. *The New York Times*, 28 Jan. 1939
3. *The New York Times,* 16 Oct. 1892